IMAGES
of America

KNOX FARM STATE PARK

On the Cover: This photograph shows the Aurora team in action on ESS KAY Farm at a well-attended game. The Aurora team's silks were blue and gold, later to become the colors of the Buffalo Sabres hockey team. ESS KAY Farm hosted many polo games over decades. Now named the Neil and Barbara Chur Equestrian Center, this field hosts both soccer and polo matches. (Photograph by and courtesy of Ric DeLaney, *Buffalo Courier-Express*.)

IMAGES
of America

KNOX FARM STATE PARK

Gerald L. Halligan and Renee M. Oubre
Foreword by Seymour Knox IV

ARCADIA
PUBLISHING

ISBN 978-0-7385-9921-2

Published by Arcadia Publishing
Charleston, South Carolina

Printed in the United States of America

Library of Congress Control Number: 2012953752

For all general information, please contact Arcadia Publishing:
Telephone 843-853-2070
Fax 843-853-0044
E-mail sales@arcadiapublishing.com
For customer service and orders:
Toll-Free 1-888-313-2665

Visit us on the Internet at www.arcadiapublishing.com

To Elizabeth Wallace, a visionary woman who embodies the spirit of the Friends of Knox Farm—she has generously given of her time and personal resources to make this book a reality.

Contents

FOREWORD

Hello,

Thank you for purchasing this terrific book on the history of Knox Farm State Park.

I have had a lifelong fascination with the Ideal Stock Farm, ESS KAY Farm, and now the historic Knox Farm State Park, ranging from riding, tennis, squash, and polo and the worldwide members of the polo community to my grandfather's health regime, which took him into his 90s; Seymour's Shangri-la (his famous Sunday lunches); and his banking and artist friends—intellectual stimulation for our community and beyond.

Growing up on the farm with my grandmother and grandfather was an idyllic childhood. Learning to swim, play tennis, croquet, Frisbee, and ride horses was a dream come true. My brothers and cousins also had a great time playing, biking through the woods, riding motorbikes through the woods, driving go-carts, and singing songs of the times.

Years later, I was married on the farm to my wonderful bride, Connie, my kids spent time there growing up, and my sister Helen was married there as well. My cousin Norty and his bride, Vickie, also exchanged vows on the farm.

In 1996, my dad passed away at the farm, as did my Uncle Norty in 1998. This soon started the quixotic tale to how the farm became a state park. If you never believed in serendipitous events, now is the time.

I hope you take the time to enjoy some of the best views of Western New York. It is beautiful no matter what time of year you visit, and I never get tired of walking there. Deer, turkeys, ducks, the occasional raccoon, and lots of squirrels are always on display.

I would like to thank my new friends Gerry Halligan and Renee Oubre for taking the initiative to put this book together. I would also like to thank Betsy Wallace and the Friends Group of Knox Farm State Park for all of their contributions.

I would also like to thank my great-grandfather, a distinguished entrepreneur of the early 20th century, for his insight into acquiring the property. He is to this day a great example for our generation and the generations ahead! A thank-you is owed to my great-grandmother Grace and her children, Dorothy, Marjorie, and Seymour, for all of their contributions to our community. Furthermore, I would like to thank my late dad and uncle for contributing so much to our community and for following in their late dad's footsteps. Notably, I would like to thank my mom, Jean, for all her hard work inmaking a great idea become a reality for so many park lovers. And finally, s grateful thanks goes to my wonderful wife, Connie, and my boys, Seymour V and Jack, for their love and support.

To whom much is given, much is expected.
Thank you and God Bless,
Seymour H. Knox IV

Acknowledgments

The book that you hold in your hands is the tangible result of the creativity and cooperation of many people who love Knox Farm State Park. Without the guidance and cooperation of the following persons and their respective organizations, this book would have not been possible: Brenda Hale, librarian, Stacie Hale, historian, and the late Marie Rocca, former historian for Russell, New York; Laura Linke, senior reference specialist, of Carl A. Kroch Library, Cornell University; William Offhaus and Michael Basinski of the State University of New York at Buffalo; Kelly Carpenter of Albright-Knox Art Gallery; Cynthia Van Ness and Amy Miller of the Buffalo History Museum; Daniel DiLandro and Peggy Hatfield of Special Collections, Butler Library at State University College at Buffalo; Amy Pickard, Charles Alaimo, and Jay Barone, Grosvenor Room at Buffalo and Erie County Central Library; George Eastman House staff, Rochester, New York; Matthew Biddle of *Western New York Heritage* magazine; Patrick Lango; Ed Abramowski, Robert Dugan, and Dennis Lynch, all affiliated with the Buffalo Bills; Ed Rutkowski, former county executive of Erie County; Kristen Kirby, *East Aurora Advertiser* editor; Robert Goller of Aurora Historical Society; Don Dayer, former East Aurora town historian; East Aurora Library staff; John Davidson of the North Star Tavern; and Patrick Montgomery for providing images from the Bert Morgan Archives.

Special thanks go to the following members of the S.H. Knox family and members of the various support organizations that have made Knox Farm State Park a reality: Jean Read Knox, whose vision initiated the effort to preserve the property; Seymour Knox IV, who supported the book from the beginning; Read Knox, Avery Knox and Nancy Knox Talcott; Helen Edith Knox, Linda Knox McLean, and Northrup Knox Jr.; John Glenn; Elizabeth Wallace of Friends of Knox Farm State Park and the Seven to Save; Sue Collins and Elizabeth O'Donnell of the East Aurora Driving Society and Dean Miller, their photographer; and the Niagara Parks Commission. For their perpetual patience, grateful thank-you is owed to Kathleen M. Halligan and Paul and Jane Oubre.

INTRODUCTION

The Knox Farm State Park is a gemstone in a collection of precious historic places throughout Western New York, both public and private, that are linked to the descendants of Seymour Horace Knox. This new park under the jurisdiction of the State of New York was a working farm and then a very private summer retreat in its early years. However, down through the decades, the landscape began to reflect the different interests of the members of the Knox family who felt this country estate was a special place.

During the last 20 years, the family and New York State began to grant access beyond the iconic stonewalls to the general public. Thus allowing others to appreciate the land and buildings previously enjoyed only by the Knox family, close friends, and business associates.

This volume will offer a very condensed version of the history of the Knox Farm and its original family that spans more than 100 years. It is a fascinating story grounded in the entrepreneurial fire of young Seymour Knox, who worked his way out of rural Russell, New York, to become one of the more notable businessmen of his era. Although the scale of his success, which by many standards would have been predicted to be impossible to achieve, Knox never forgot his roots.

In order to appreciate this, one must travel to Russell, New York, to view the beautiful testament to his love for his mother, Jane E. Knox. In the early 1900s, Seymour H. Knox had a building constructed and three Tiffany stained-glass windows were placed in the Knox Memorial School to commemorate her memory. At the bottom of the middle panel is a simple inscription. The original building was sold, and the windows were moved to their present location in the foyer of the local high school.

The creation of the Knox Farm State Park captures this same spirit. The flow of images allows the reader to visit the three principal groups of buildings while enjoying a wide range of natural features.

One

It All Begins in Russell, New York

Seymour H. Knox was the son of James Horace Knox and Jane E. McBrier of Russell, New York. After attending the local district school, he became a teacher at the young age of 15; Seymour did not go to high school. After a few years, Knox traveled to Hart, Michigan, to work as a salesclerk. With experience under his belt, he decided to partner with one of his relatives from Pennsylvania in a general merchandise store. This venture did not succeed, but this did not deter Knox.

With funds loaned to him from his mother's life savings, Knox and his cousin Woolworth jointly opened a five-and-dime store in Reading, Pennsylvania, in 1884. Although the store had a slow start, it would serve as the foundation for a chain of stores that would flourish in the Northeast. Knox founded his first store in Buffalo, New York, on Main Street in 1888.

Knox further diversified his business interests and in 1912 collaborated with his cousins Frank W. Woolworth and Charles Woolworth. He merged his 112 stores into the corporation known as F.W. Woolworth Company of five-and-dime stores to secure his fortune. While holding leadership status within Woolworths, Knox was also involved with the Marine Trust Company, one of the prominent banking institutions in Western New York.

While becoming established in Buffalo, Knox married Grace Millard in 1890, and their family grew with the birth of four children: Gracia, who died in infancy; Dorothy; Seymour Jr.; and Marjorie. Knox's love of horses took him to the town of East Aurora, New York, which was the center for breeding trotters and pacers. He purchased several adjoining farms and secured some horses for his stock from the Hamlin Farm sale. Several were from the lineage of Mambrino King, reputed to be the finest champion of the era.

The sprawling property along Seneca Street was named the Ideal Stock Farm. The character of the summer retreat influenced the Knox children, and its organic features started to shape the destiny of following generations.

Seymour H. Knox's first stores with his cousin F.W. Woolworth were not very profitable. After separating, Knox created a chain of stores in his own right. In 1912, Knox, F.W. Woolworth, F.M. Kirby, E.P. Charlton, and C.S. Woolworth merged into one corporation. Knox only lived three more years and did not see the worldwide success of the merger. (Courtesy of the Seymour H. Knox family.)

This building served as an arsenal for the War of 1812 and later became a school in the village of Russell. Since it was the only local school for many years, several generations of children carved their initials on its walls and rafters, including "S.H.K." for Seymour H. Knox. Seymour received his early education there. The structure was destroyed by fire in March 1945. (Courtesy of Russell Historical Society.)

Although most of the young businessmen in this photograph are unidentified, Seymour H. Knox is at the extreme right. This image was found in a loose collection of prints with the inscription written on the back: "Knox, who are your friends—Armstrong." (Courtesy of the Seymour H. Knox family.)

Seymour H. Knox opened his first store in Buffalo in 1888. The view shows the southeast corner of Main and Clinton Streets. The Knox store was just to the right of the store on the corner. (The George Nathan Newman Collection of Photographs of Vanished and Vanishing Buffalo, courtesy of Buffalo and Erie County Central Library.)

The city block that contained the Knox store was destroyed by fire on December 14, 1893. Knox simply moved his store down the street to another location. This is now the site of the Brisbane Building. (The George Nathan Newman Collection of Photographs of Vanished and Vanishing Buffalo, courtesy of Buffalo and Erie County Central Library.)

In 1890, Seymour H. Knox bought out F.W. Woolworth's interests in Erie, Buffalo, and Lockport. With his increasing success, he expanded his presence in other nearby states. This image is from the store in Toledo, Ohio. (Courtesy of the Seymour H. Knox family.)

These are formal portraits of Seymour H. Knox and his wife, Grace Millard. Originally from Detroit, Michigan, Grace endowed the University at Buffalo, enabling its establishment. She founded the Junior League of Buffalo, whose Decorators Showhouse is at the main house of Knox Farm State Park in 2013. She also supported the Albright Gallery and the Buffalo Museum of Science. (Both, courtesy of the Seymour H. Knox family.)

Seymour and Grace were blessed with four children. The first child, Gracia, died when she was about two years old. The other children were Dorothy, Seymour Jr., and Marjorie. The children had a wonderful time together. Note that Seymour is holding Marjorie's hand in the picture. (Courtesy of Northrup Knox Jr.)

Seymour H. Knox was a lover of art and presented many beautiful pictures to the Albright Gallery. His private collection is one of the finest in Buffalo, as noted in his obituary on May 18, 1915. He also was director of the Philharmonic Society of Buffalo. (Courtesy of the Albright-Knox Art Gallery.)

This 1909 impressionistic oil painting by Harrington Mann is titled *Portrait of Three Knox Children*. It features Dorothy, Marjorie, and Seymour Jr. with their springer spaniel. The painting was a gift in 1970 to the Albright-Knox Art Gallery from Seymour H. Knox Jr., Marjorie K.C. Klopp, and Dorothy K.G. Rogers. (Courtesy of the Albright-Knox Art Gallery.)

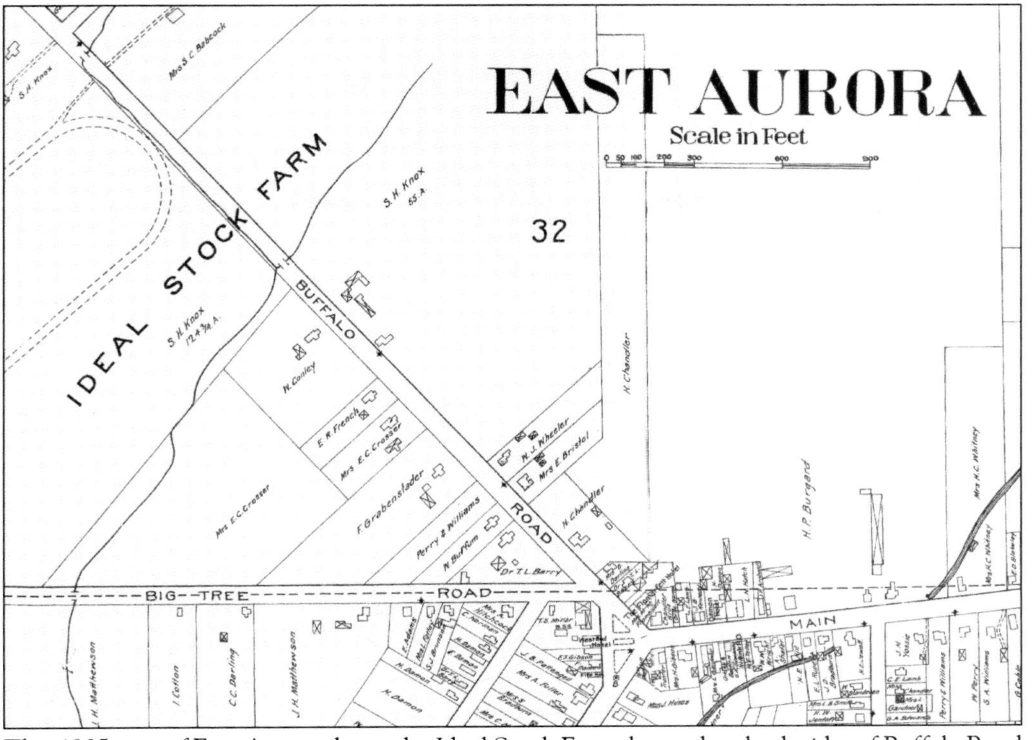

This 1905 map of East Aurora shows the Ideal Stock Farm, located on both sides of Buffalo Road (Seneca Street). It included 124.75 acres on the south side and 65 acres to the north. (Courtesy of the Aurora Historical Society.)

Knox purchased a farm in East Aurora, about 16 miles south of Buffalo, New York, as a place that he could enjoy his hobbies and recreation. In those times, this was quite a distance to drive along dirt roads. According to family records, Knox would pack up the family, including their dogs, around July 1, travel to the farm, and stay until autumn. (Courtesy of the Aurora Historical Society.)

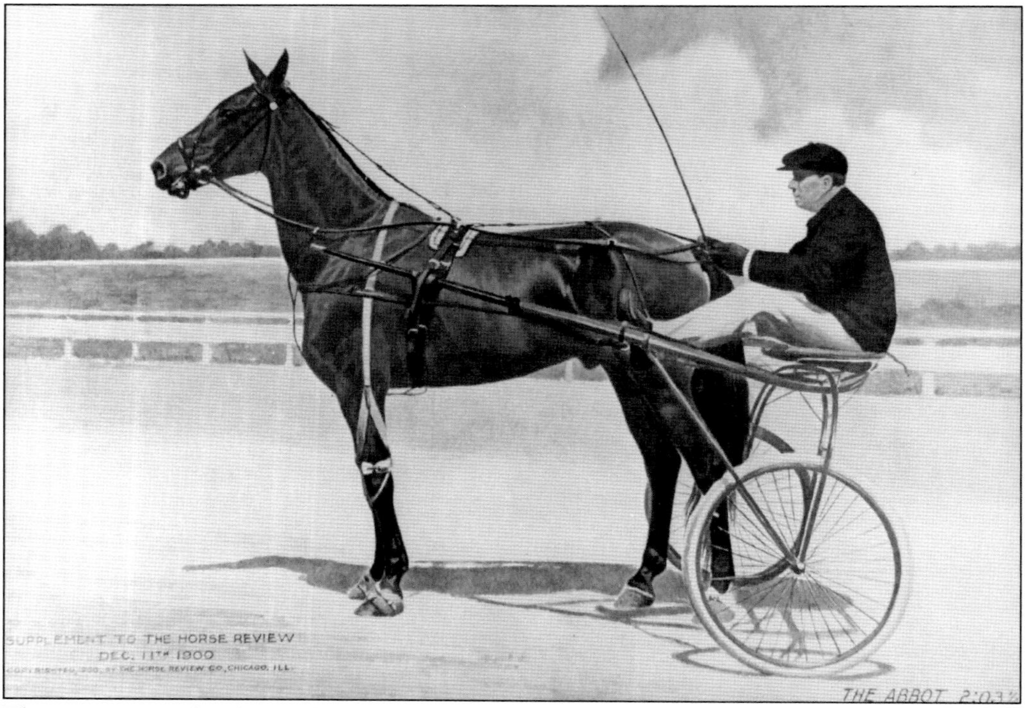

This is an example of one of the fine trotters, shown in full racing harness, from the Hamlin Farm. In 1880, East Aurora was home to the world's largest covered racetrack that burned to the ground a year after it was built. Knox had a training track on the Ideal Stock Farm. (Courtesy of the Aurora Historical Society.)

One of his intentions was to breed Standardbred racehorses. The name chosen for the property, Ideal Stock Farm, was derived from his first stallion, Prince Ideal. The auction records show that the purchase was the surprise of the event with Knox paying $10,000 for the horse. This is an unidentified horse from Knox's breeding stock. (Courtesy of the Seymour H. Knox family.)

The Ideal Stock Farm stables were built to accommodate about 40 horses with a half-mile dirt track for training and a small cinder track for wet weather. Paul White was the principal trainer who developed champion pacers. The best known of these was The Abbe, who sired many future winners. This brood mare was found in a collection of Knox horse photographs. (Courtesy of the Seymour H. Knox family.)

Pictured here ready for a sleigh ride is Seymour Knox with his wife, Grace, and friends. Sleighs were very important during this era due to limited road accessibility during heavy snowfalls in Western New York. On the farm in the dairy barn is a collection of carriages and sleighs from that time period. (Courtesy of the Russell Historical Museum.)

This is a rare photograph of Seymour Knox holding his daughter Dorothy. The girl in the rocking chair is unidentified. The location of the house is unknown; however, it may have been the original home on the Ideal Stock Farm, which was torn down in the 1930s. (Courtesy of the Seymour H. Knox family.)

Seymour H. Knox served as a teacher in the district's schools as a young man. On July 30, 1913, the Knox Memorial School was dedicated as a gift by Knox for Russell. In remembrance of Jane E. Knox, his mother, Knox had a Tiffany stained-glass window installed in this school. The windows are now in the new Edwards-Knox School in Russell, New York. (Courtesy of Russell Historical Society.)

This photograph is of the wake of Seymour Knox at their home on Delaware Avenue in Buffalo. Copious flowers are from friends and business associates worldwide. Seymour H. Knox's portrait hangs above the mantel. Funeral attendees included John J. Albright, A. Conger Goodyear, Charles S. Woolworth, and George F. Rand. (Courtesy of the Seymour H. Knox family.)

The Knox mausoleum is on Mirror Lake in Forest Lawn Cemetery, Buffalo, New York. The mausoleums of Knox and his business associates are in close proximity to one another. These include Daniel Good, who he partnered with in the five-and-dime business in 1905. (Courtesy of the Seymour H. Knox family.)

Grace Millard Knox is pictured at her 806 Delaware Avenue mansion following the death of her husband. She was very supportive of her son's interest in polo and shared her husband's love of horses. She adored being amidst close friends and family. Grace Knox passed onto her reward in 1936. (Courtesy of the Seymour H. Knox family.)

Two

The Residences, Pool, and Squash Court

Seymour Jr. began to take his own place as major decision maker of the farm with the purchase of his sister Dorothy's home on the East Aurora property in 1929. Knox transformed the buildings and property to match his own dreams. He changed the name to ESS KAY Farm to memorialize his father.

Like his father, Knox Jr. wanted to maintain an agricultural system that was multifunctional and self-sustaining. With no interest in racing horses, Knox changed the main track to a polo field. The main barns were then converted to care for hunters used in East Aurora and Aiken, South Carolina, horse events. The family had a winter home in Aiken.

On the property's northeastern edge was the original farmhouse that was torn down in the 1930s. There are several residential buildings on the estate, occupied seasonally in the early years, then year-round as the needs of the farm changed. The main house was constructed between 1916 and 1917 by Dorothy and her husband, Frank H. Goodyear Jr. Cleveland-based architects Frank Bell Meade and James Montgomery Hamilton designed this flagship two-story summer home.

In 1929, the Goodyears sold the summer home to Seymour H. Knox Jr. Tragically, on October 14, 1930, thirty-nine-year-old Frank Goodyear died in an automobile accident. Dorothy Goodyear carried on following his passing and later married Edmund Pendleton Rogers.

An addition, including a playroom, was built onto the main house in 1934. That same year, the squash courts, garages, and dog kennels were erected adjacent to the main house. The guesthouse was constructed for visitors of Knox Jr., such as polo players, hunting companions, and business associates, and has four bedrooms and four bathrooms. In 1953, it was remodeled with additions constructed on each end of the building that included a porch, living room, master bedroom, and a garage. After that year, it became the home of Northrup and Lucetta Knox and their children. Northrup, the second son of Seymour H. Knox Jr., lived in this home for 50 years.

Young Seymour Knox Jr. is pictured in a fine suit and tie. He attended the Nichols School in Buffalo and the Hotchkiss School in Connecticut. He attended Yale University, graduating in 1920. While there, he was a member of Delta Kappa Epsilon. (Courtesy of Northrup Knox Jr..)

Pictured here in 1905 is the lovely Helen Northrup at the age of three. She was born in Buffalo, the daughter of Louis G. and Sara E. Northrup. She attended Lafayette High School and the Albright Art School in Buffalo, New York. She married Seymour Knox Jr. Many of her fine paintings hung in the main house on ESS KAY Farm. (Courtesy of the Seymour H. Knox family.)

In February 1917, while a freshman at Yale University, Seymour Knox Jr. (second row, fourth from right) joined the Yale 2nd Division in response to German submarine attacks on Allied merchant ships in World War I. Tragically, on May 30, 1917, while on training flight in Buffalo, New York, the Curtiss F-Boat crashed, killing the pilot Fred Zimmer and severely injured Knox. This ended his participation in the war effort. (Courtesy of the Seymour H. Knox family.)

This image, titled "On the Fence," was taken in Seymour's graduating year at Yale, indicating that he was captain of the squash team in 1920. Squash was the sporting activity that rivaled polo on ESS KAY Farm. The family later built a squash court on the property. Many of the family members played; Seymour III and Northrup were recognized national champions. (Courtesy of the Seymour H. Knox family.)

This formal portrait is of Dorothy Knox Goodyear, who was responsible for developing the new residences on the ESS KAY Farm. She and her husband, Frank H. Goodyear, sold the property to her brother Seymour around 1929. In the early 1930s, Frank Goodyear died tragically in a car accident. Dorothy was later married to Edmund Rogers. (Photograph by Clara Sipprell; courtesy of the Seymour H. Knox family.)

This photograph shows the original entrance to ESS KAY Farm with an elegant wrought iron gate and stone fence. Driving on Seneca Street, one instantly recognizes Knox Farm by this iconic sculptured gate. The road through this gate leads to the main house and the stables. (Photograph by and courtesy of Peter Potter.)

The main house was built as a 14,400-square-foot, two-story summer home between 1916 and 1917. It looks out on one of the most beautiful vistas in the park. The home enjoys good ventilation due to its location and position on the top of the hill. (Courtesy of the Seymour H. Knox family.)

At one time, elm trees that provided shade in the heat of summer surrounded the main house. Trees, especially native species, were important in the Shipman garden plans for the property; Ellen Biddle Shipman designed the exterior gardens and formal estate grounds. (Courtesy of the Seymour H. Knox family.)

This view is from the garden toward the main house's screened porch; above it is a sleeping porch that has three windowed sides. In one of the bedrooms, there is a set of bookshelves on either side of a fireplace. One of the bookshelves serves as a hidden door to the sleeping porch. (Courtesy of the Seymour H. Knox family.)

The main house boasts an art studio with tiled floor and north light. Upstairs in the main house are sleeping quarters for the family. Walking the hallway from the family bedrooms to quarters for the help, one must descend three steps. This was to indicate status, according to English manor style. (Courtesy of the Seymour H. Knox family.)

Helen Northrup Knox is seen here with her two boys, Seymour Knox III and Northrup, on the steps of the grass terrace in front of the porch. The balustrade shown in this image was dismantled in recent years due to deterioration. (Courtesy of the Seymour H. Knox family.)

Among the photographic images on the wall in the Ping-Pong Room, is the picture of Seymour Knox Jr. on his horse Vanity Fair. He is being congratulated by his wife, Helen, and sister Marjorie after winning the polo pony race held just before the polo match against the Dayton team. The event was held at ESS KAY Farm in 1927. (Photograph by and courtesy of Renee Oubre.)

Another photographic image on the opposite wall in the Ping-Pong Room is this view taken during a match between the Buffalo Country Club and Meadowbrook in July 1923. Seymour Knox Jr. is mounted on Ping-Pong, and Devereux Milburn is in the background to the right. Seymour Knox IV said that KODAK processed these wall-sized photographs. (Photograph by and courtesy of Renee Oubre.)

Here is Seymour H. Knox Jr. with his wife, Helen, and sons Seymour III and Northrup. This early-1930s photograph was made during the time Seymour was establishing himself in the business world and redefining the character of the farm. (Courtesy of the Seymour H. Knox family.)

The family felines made their way onto the photographic wallpaper of the Ping-Pong Room. The one on the right was named Mister Mewmy. The Knoxes displayed their beloved horses, dogs, and cats in these sepia images, preserving fond memories. (Courtesy of the Seymour H. Knox family.)

This fireplace holds French-made porcelain fagots, which, after being heated, radiate warmth into the room. Above the stylish mantel is a portrait of Helen Northrup Knox, which appeared in a major national magazine. (Courtesy of the Seymour H. Knox family.)

This room is referred to as the middle living room. It has wonderful views of the grounds. Among the many interesting details of the room are decoupage lamps and needlepoint pillows, handmade by Jean Knox. These were on view during tours of the main house given in 1999. (Photograph by Jean Knox; courtesy of the Seymour H. Knox family.)

This is the breakfast room that looks out over the terrace. It was used not only for breakfast but for most of the informal family meals. Off this room to the left is the pantry area of the kitchen that is used for storing china and other serving pieces. (Courtesy of the Seymour H. Knox family.)

Ready playmates, the cousins breakfast together after gathering fresh brown eggs with Grampa in the Rolls-Royce. Seated at the table are Linda, Seymour, Read, Norty Knox, and Gaye Flickenger. (Courtesy of the Seymour H. Knox family.)

Walking past the main house, one comes upon a second, smaller home with yellow shutters. This was the original guesthouse that later became the home of Northrup and his family. (Courtesy of the Seymour H. Knox family.)

The Shipman gardens are visible from the guesthouse. The house is at the end of the main access road in close proximity to the pool house. Among shade trees and knolls, it is sweetly nestled in privacy and is an easy walk to the main house. (Courtesy of the Seymour H. Knox family.)

Young Norty and Linda, on the walkway, pick flowers from the side garden of their home. The yard opens onto a pasture that provides a sweeping view of the woods on Knox Road. (Courtesy of the Seymour H. Knox family.)

Lucetta is seen here with her children Linda and Norty enjoying the fine weather. Lucetta was an active participant in daily life on the farm, and she was well liked by the farm employees. (Courtesy of the Seymour H. Knox family.)

Frolicking at the pool with a toy sailboat, Seymour IV makes a splash. Looking on is one of the ubiquitous spaniels. (Courtesy of the Seymour H. Knox family.)

Norty was a very happy little boy perched on the diving board, holding the mast of a toy sailboat, perhaps ready to launch it at his cousin Sey IV. The swimming pool was a major center of relaxation and entertainment for visitors. (Courtesy of the Seymour H. Knox family.)

The pool house was constructed in the late 1950s or early 1960s. The water came from a spring in one of the pastures, and because it was very cold, a heater was installed soon afterward. Inside the pool house were hung favorite paintings from Seymour Knox Jr.'s private collection. The pool house was the setting for many of Seymour Knox Jr.'s Sunday lunches. (Courtesy of the Seymour H. Knox family.)

Pictured at the rear of the pool house after one of the Knoxes' traditional Sunday lunches are children Heather Flickenger, Helen Edith, Avery, and Seymour Knox IV. Pine trees were added by Ellen Biddle Shipman, who felt it was important to have white pines and hemlock because she believed them to be very beautiful and native. (Courtesy of the Seymour H. Knox family.)

Frederick C. Bachus built the squash courts in 1934. Bachus served as official architect for the City of Buffalo and was the architect of the first public housing project in 1939. The housing project was recognized as one of the best modern buildings in the Buffalo area. (Courtesy of Austin Corbett.)

The Knoxes enjoyed playing racquet sports. Seymour H. Knox Jr. won the city singles tournament, and his son Seymour III won the National Squash Singles in Buffalo during the 1970s. An article in *Sports Illustrated*, titled "School of Hard Knox," pictured both Seymour III and Northrup in the year that Northrup was world champion in court tennis in 1959. He retired 10 years undefeated. (Courtesy of Austin Corbett.)

Three

Lord & Burnham Greenhouse and Shipman Gardens

Helen Knox loved the greenhouse and spent many hours cultivating her plants throughout her years at ESS KAY Farm. Among her favorites were tomatoes, carrots, and many varieties of flowers. The glass-enclosed portion of the main greenhouse was twice the length it is today. It was designed and built in 1927 for the Goodyears by Frederick A. Lord and William Addison Burnham. The noted boiler and greenhouse manufacturer became associated with major public conservatories in the United States in the early 1900s.

The Knoxes wanted a greenhouse in order to have fresh produce year-round. Two full-time gardeners were hired to manage it. One practical feature of the tower roofline is the little opening for pigeons. With the birds roosting in the tower, the gardeners were able to collect their droppings and combine them with straw to help fertilize the gardens. Secondly, pigeon and squabs were used in sport hunting outings.

Nearby, the gardener's cottage housed the head gardener. Later, it was also home to the farm manager. An addition was put on during years that Northrup Knox lived on the farm, as a home for his cook.

Ellen Biddle Shipman (1869–1950) designed the exterior gardens and formal estate grounds. Shipman was highly regarded as a premier American landscape architect for her attention to personal detail and lush planting style. In 1933, *House and Garden* magazine declared her the "Dean of Women Landscape Architects."

The archive at Cornell University preserves many letters of correspondence between Ellen Biddle Shipman and Seymour and Helen Knox Jr. regarding details of seasonal planting, garden maintenance, and adjustments in the basic design of landscape. These indicate that Shipman maintained a very personal interest in those families who incorporated her design elements into their estates for many years following the initial plantings.

Shipman toured and lectured extensively, and records indicate that she completed over 400 projects on many notable homes and estates. On the Knox property, the floral enhancements are clean and direct with exacting selection of hardy woody shrubs that do well in the short seasons of the Niagara frontier. The small gardens with walking lanes near the main house invoked a sense of peace and refinement.

The Lord & Burnham greenhouse is a charming building designed and constructed by the renowned designer and architect team. This famous duo, Lord & Burnham, designed the beautiful Buffalo and Erie County Botanical Gardens. (Photograph by and courtesy of Renee Oubre.)

The family had a greenhouse built on the estate so that they could grow fresh produce and flowers year-round. Jean Knox noted that flowers were regularly sent to Aiken, South Carolina, where the family had a winter home. (Courtesy of the Seymour H. Knox family.)

Avery Knox was an avid photographer who chronicled scenes and events on ESS KAY Farm. He captured images of flowers from his grandmother's greenhouse and garden. He later published two books of images on Seymour Knox Jr. at ESS KAY Farm. (Courtesy of the Seymour H. Knox family.)

Helen Northrup Knox did not want the Shipman garden to survive her. Two years before she passed away, she requested that the garden be plowed under. All that remains of it are the yew, white pine, hemlock, and the daffodil that dot the landscape. (Courtesy of the Seymour H. Knox family.)

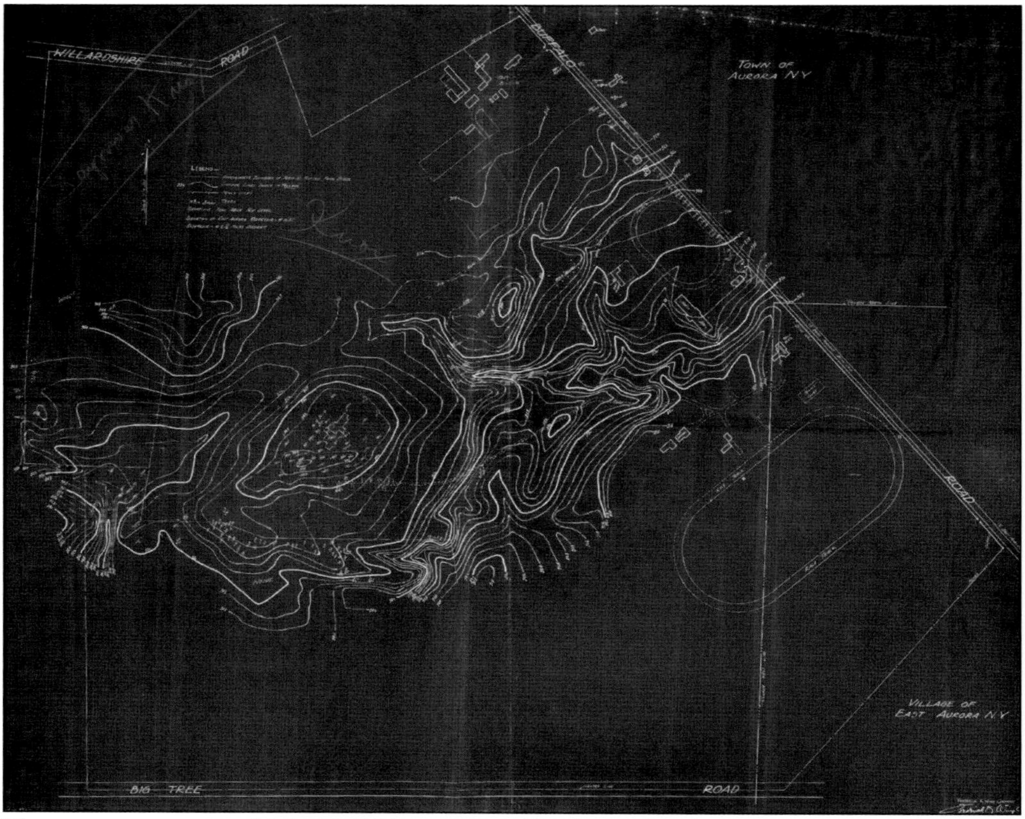

This contour map, dated July 16, 1916, was created by the Frederick K. Wing Company of Buffalo, New York, and was used by Ellen Biddle Shipman for landscape design planning for the ESS KAY Farm. Shipman placed her stamp on the back of it, indicating that it was received July 30, 1930. (Courtesy of Division of Rare and Manuscript Collections, Carl A. Kroch Library, Cornell University.)

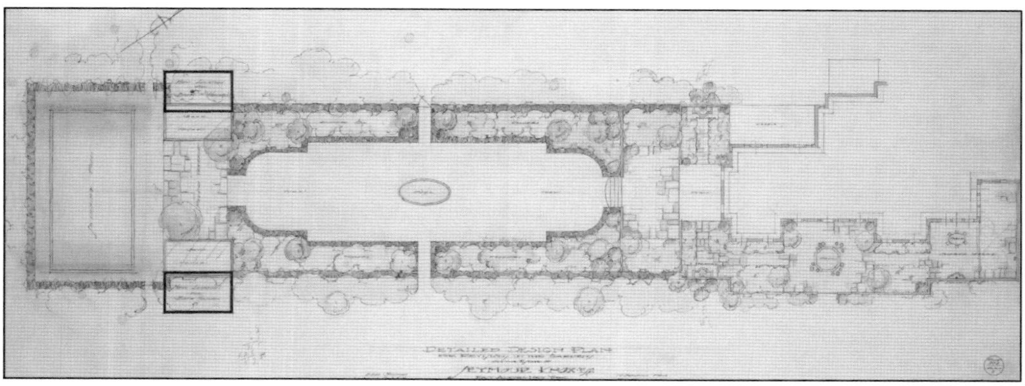

This image shows "the detailed design plan for revisions in the gardens on the estate of Seymour Knox, Esq., East Aurora, New York, August 1931." One of Shipman's strengths that set her apart from many of her peers was her extensive knowledge of plants. (Courtesy of Division of Rare and Manuscript Collections, Carl A. Kroch Library, Cornell University.)

This is a 1930s portrait of the renowned landscape architect Ellen Biddle Shipman by Frederick Bradley of New York. This date is an estimate because the photograph appears in a March 13, 1938, *New York Times* article accompanying the original print. (Courtesy of Division of Rare and Manuscript Collections, Carl A. Kroch Library, Cornell University.)

One of Shipman's challenges was seeking to achieve the "perpetual-bloom effect" to carry through the growing seasons. She conveys this in her planting directives but delves more into it through her correspondence with her clients. Selections of certain plants and their composition are carefully explained based on the seasonal conditions of the site and the gardening skills of the clients. (Courtesy of the Seymour H. Knox family.)

It should be noted that some of the landscape design work that Shipman did on ESS KAY Farm came in the twilight years of her career, which spanned 1912 through 1947. Her personal letters to both Seymour and Helen Knox during the years 1945 and 1946 reflect an ongoing dialogue about the gardens with a mutual level of respect. (Courtesy of the Seymour H. Knox family.)

The flower garden edging and borders were meticulously planned in color, number, type, height, and time of seasonal bloom. Factored in was the flowers' visual interplay with larger shrubs and trees, as each was placed near the man-made structures. This is seen in Shipman's notes about yews that were moved to hide the service courts near the squash building. (Courtesy of the Seymour H. Knox family.)

In the primary landscape preparations of her planting directives, Shipman attempted to project how certain views would be established. She also anticipated for her client how the view might change as the land and house plantings matured. In one particular letter, Shipman comments that if a hedgerow is removed, the road behind it might need to be lowered to remove it from the view from the front terrace. (Courtesy of Rare and Manuscript Collection, Carl A. Kroch Library, Cornell University.)

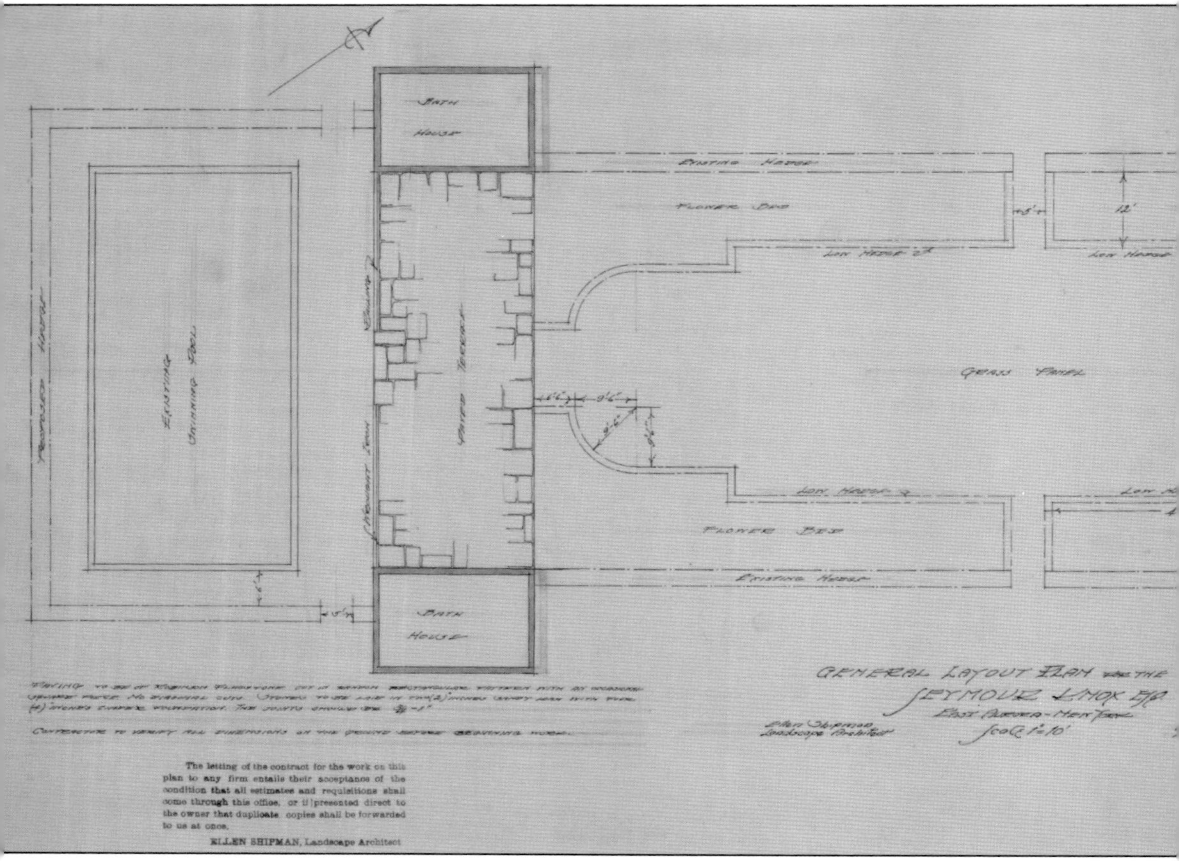

This image shows the progression in Shipman's planning process a few months later. In one of her letters, she identifies this as "The General Layout plan for the garden of Seymour Knox, Esq., East Aurora, New York, November 1931." Her drawings and written plans reflect how individual

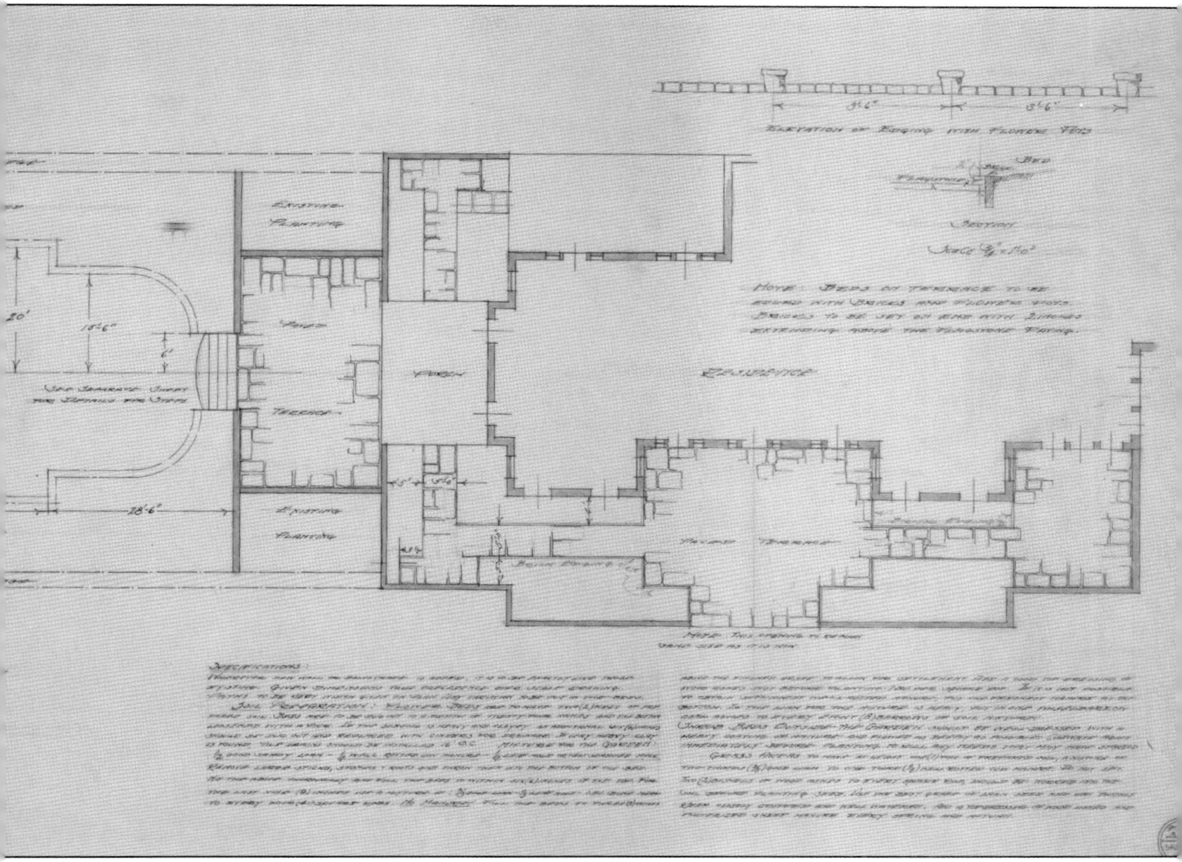

plants would grow and bloom when mixed together, based on their particular genus and specific care requirements. (Courtesy of Division of Rare and Manuscript Collections, Carl A. Kroch Library, Cornell University.)

The flowers, trees, and grounds found on Knox Farm State Park reflect the relationship that Seymour and Helen Knox had with Ellen Biddle Shipman. It was a creative partnership that refined a rural pastureland into a landscape of contentment and peace. Although current visitors have to use their imaginations to envision the Shipman gardens, perhaps one day the gardens will be restored to their elegance of former times. (Courtesy of the Seymour H. Knox family.)

Peonies, named after the figure Paeon in Greek mythology, were among the dominant plants in the garden's layout. Planted in front of them were 15 varieties of complimentary flowers in a wide range of color. These included several types of bellflowers of blue and purple, asters, white alyssum, alkanets, garland roses in pink, common rockroses, forget-me-nots, catmints, and bright yellow sundrops. (Courtesy of the Seymour H. Knox family.)

To the rear near the back edge of the garden, Shipman chose taller plants to fill empty spaces near the peonies. Among these were four types of German iris, Russell lupines, Oriental poppies, and three different campanula blossoms. Features that were important to Shipman included the iris's ability to bloom early in the spring and its deer-resistant quality that it shares with the lupines. (Courtesy of the Seymour H. Knox family.)

In a letter dated June 26, 1945, Shipman advises the following: "In early September give large peony 1 qt bone meal around the outer roots. After the ground has frozen and the peonies cut back, cover the plant with well rotted cow manure. This can form a mulch for the following season." (Courtesy of the Seymour H. Knox family.)

Also in her correspondence, Shipman suggests the use of six-inch flowerpots to cover new plantings. "Use well rotted cow manure, sharp sand and a little limestone over a bed of coarse gravel or coarse sand (as base). Break a hole in the bottom of the pot and place it over the young plant letting the top come through." (Courtesy of the Seymour H. Knox family.)

In the following, Shipman responds to a question regarding a particular flower: "The plant with blue flowers you (Knox) asked about in the Campbell garden is Spiderwort, the flowers close in the afternoon. I did not put it in as I never use it on that account and it gets very straggly." (Courtesy of the Seymour H. Knox family.)

Shipman suggests, "Take out the hedge behind the playhouse if this hides a road. Keep the hedge until the road can be dropped so that it will not show in the view from the terrace. Also take out the arbor vitae under the elms by the terrace." (Courtesy of the Seymour H. Knox family.)

On August 8, Shipman recommends honeysuckle from Wayside Gardens in Ohio in response to a Knox question. She says, "The vines are best planted in the spring, but if planted in autumn, they may go through the winter alright with protection. The soil should be 18 inches deep with 1/3 well rotted cow manure and 2/3 topsoil." (Courtesy of the Seymour H. Knox family.)

In planting vegetables, Shipman's grasp of good horticultural practice is clear. Applicable to vegetables as well as ornamental plants, Shipman recommends crimson clover seed to fertilize the soil prior to planting. (Courtesy of the Seymour H. Knox family.)

The following are her comments about the prospective view from the front terrace: "At left, take out or cut down all the evergreens around the two maples, so you can get a view of the big elm and the field in the distance. Cut down more to see the stream in the distance." (Courtesy of the Seymour H. Knox family.)

Four

Livestock Barns

Seymour Knox purchased the Wallenwein Dairy Farm, including a pre–Civil War barn that is still seen on the farm today. Originally built on the ground, it was later rolled onto a fieldstone foundation. Aberdeen Angus cattle were kept in the bull shed attached to this barn. Next to that is the heifer barn. The last barn constructed on the Knox property in the 1940s, the heifer barn was finished inside with fine wood to help entice prospective buyers of Angus cattle.

The show barn was used specifically for foxhounds for the East Aurora Hunt Club. The kennels have hound doors in the foundation. In later years, this barn was used to prepare cattle for fairs, shows, and sales. A short distance away is the sheep barn, which originally housed cattle. The sheep barn was rebuilt after a 1951 fire. On the top floor of this barn, chickens were raised, with hens on one side and chicks on the other.

Next door in the milk house, raw milk was processed with a foot-operated milk churn. To the rear was the icehouse. In winter, ice blocks were cut from the ponds by hand and brought to the building by sleigh. Ice was stored in sawdust on the dirt floor of the icehouse to preserve milk. Later, the dirt floor was replaced with a hardwood floor as refrigeration came into use. Upstairs were living quarters for farm employees.

The farm office barn was originally constructed as a repair shop for the horse-drawn vehicles. Northrup Knox directed operations from here. The interior walls of the structure are lined with wood from other demolished barns on the property. Across the way stands the machine and storage shed, currently used as a storage and repair shop.

Designated team barns stabled draft horses and stored hay, straw, and horse-drawn vehicles. Upstairs were living quarters for the teamsters assigned to drive teams of workhorses. When the property was acquired in 1890, the team barn was located near the gate but later was moved nearer to the other barns. Due to its deteriorated condition, the team barn was taken down in 2011.

The ESS KAY Farm is seen here in the 1960s. This view shows many barns and other buildings that have since been torn down, such as the teamster barn, the chicken coop, partridge coop, a silo, and corncrib. (Courtesy of Niagara Parks Commission.)

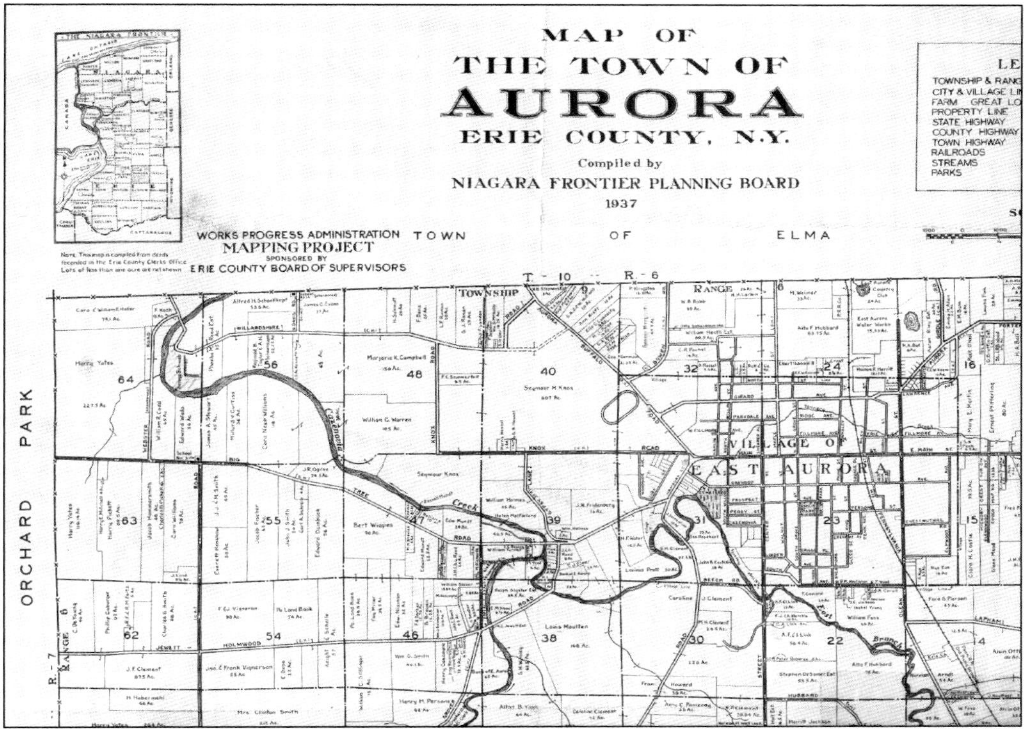

Pastures on ESS KAY Farm were enlarged with increased acreage, as seen in this map from 1937. Hay and oats were still being grown, but winter barley was added. Conversion to mechanized operations with tractors replaced the teams of workhorses. The barn that housed these horses was dismantled in recent years due to foundation deterioration. (Courtesy of the Aurora Historical Society)

This image shows the Rolls in the foreground with a complete view of the main barns, including the team barn to the extreme right. Grandchildren remember Seymour Jr. driving them around the farm in the Rolls while the dogs jumped in and out of the car. (Courtesy of the Seymour H. Knox family.)

As time passed, the focus of operations changed, and so dairy cattle were dispersed and replaced by Aberdeen Angus beef cattle. In the early 1930s, the farm's name was changed to ESS KAY Farm, using the initials of Seymour H. Knox I. The family never tired of seeing the herd of black cattle in the pastures with the light of the setting sun. (Courtesy of Seymour H. Knox family.)

The ubiquitous split rail fence runs along the border of a sunlit pasture where cattle graze. Many of the pastures were named after employees and friends. In the distance are the maintenance shed, chicken coop, and, behind it, the team barn. (Courtesy of the Seymour H. Knox family.)

A small flock of Southdown sheep was raised for roast lamb and lamb chops. During this period, chickens supplied brown eggs that were favored by Knox, but the hogs and pigs were dropped from the livestock holdings. Wild ducks and geese were welcome visitors to the farm's ponds, which also attracted fowl from nearby farms. After the park was established, sheep again grazed on the lawn, and visitors adored them. An annual fiber fest was held in the fall. (Both, courtesy of the Seymour H. Knox family.)

The main business of ESS KAY Farm was breeding Aberdeen Angus cattle. With Maynard Pangborn as farm manager, a small herd of 50 brood cows was chosen carefully. The bull calves were designated as future 4-H Club steers. The ones with particular features were placed for sale, and the others were reserved for butchering. Here, employees are walking the cattle from pasture to pasture. (Courtesy of the Seymour H. Knox family.)

The Angus heifers, which are cows that have not had calves, were sold privately on the farm and at public sales. Records indicate that prospective buyers would often fly onto the farm, landing on the polo field. Some of the other heifers were kept to replenish the main herd. (Courtesy of the Seymour H. Knox family.)

According to the writings of Seymour Knox Jr., ESS KAY Farm never gained great prominence in breeding the Aberdeen Angus cattle. However, the heifer ESS KAY Maid of Bummer 32, sold to Ankony Farms, produced a calf that became the Grand Champion Bull in Chicago in 1966. (Courtesy of the Seymour H. Knox family.)

In the latter years of raising the Aberdeen Angus, ESS KAY Farm introduced a Charolais bull into the breeding program. This breed of white cattle, originating in France, are raised for its meat and recognized for desirable qualities when crossed with other breeds. The results of this were encouraging for the herd at ESS KAY Farm. (Courtesy of the Seymour H. Knox family.)

The original dairy barn housed about 20 milk cows of the Aryshire red and white breed. Milking was done by hand in those days. The *East Aurora Advertiser* featured an article in 1913 about a remarkable amount of milk produced by a particular cow in the Ideal herd. It seems that this gained Knox a new reputation in the cattle industry. (Photograph by and courtesy of Peter Potter.)

The foxhounds used in the East Aurora Hunt were housed in this barn. There once were shade trees on one side of the barn, which kept the hounds cool in the heat of summer. It became known as the show barn, as it was used in later years to prepare cattle for shows, sales, and fairs. Major buyers descended on the farm to purchase the prized black-angus cattle. (Photograph by and courtesy of Peter Potter.)

Five

Stables and Horses

An elegant wrought iron gate stands as the former formal entrance to the farm. When Seymour Knox Jr. moved onto the property, his mother, Grace, did not want the polo ponies to be stabled with the other horses, and so a separate barn was constructed to accommodate them. Today, this little white barn is known as the guest stables and is located on the western side of the larger polo barn. The architect of the stable was Buffalo-based Harvey Staring Horton. He had designed several notable buildings in Western New York and played a significant role in the architectural scene locally.

During the late 1920s and 1930s, polo had its golden years in the United States. It is a very demanding sport for both horse and rider, requiring high levels of fitness, quick decision-making skills, and courage to gallop full out in order to score. The impressive polo barn, sometimes referred to as the summer stable, was built in 1927 in compound style, influenced by Old English country estate buildings. Knox Jr. was an international polo enthusiast who dedicated polo as one of the primary uses of the property. ESS KAY Farm served as the Aurora team's training center and as the host for local matches against area teams. Personal letters from Knox Jr. to his sons Seymour III and Northrup written prior to a major national-level competition held in Oakbrook, Illinois, in 1956, reveal his observations and suggestions for their preparation to compete at that level.

The Aurora team also competed internationally from the 1930s right through to the 1960s. ESS KAY Farm had designated handlers for polo ponies and also equipment and vehicles for long-distance transport. Seasonally, the horses were kept at ESS KAY Farm in summer but then were sent by rail to the winter estate in Aiken, South Carolina. This Southern home served as a staging base for traveling by ship to competitions in England. Some of the more famous matches for the Aurora team were held in Buenos Aires, Argentina.

On horseback in front of the original stables are Seymour Jr. and Helen Knox. Grace Knox preferred that polo ponies not to be kept with her hunters and told her son if he wanted to play polo, he would have to build his own stable. With the construction of the large stables, this became the guest stables for visiting polo teams. (Courtesy of the Seymour H. Knox family.)

From left to right are the kennel, guest stable, and polo stable with its very distinctive cupola. The cupola is no longer on the structure. The large stable's roof was made of slate in order to be fireproof. (Courtesy of the Seymour H. Knox family.)

ESS KAY Farm provided training for jumping and polo in national and foreign competition. Helen Knox is shown in this photograph jumping a Hitchcock-style fence riding sidesaddle. This photograph was most likely taken in Aiken, South Carolina. Thomas Hitchcock Sr. built a famous steeplechase training track on their property in Aiken. (Courtesy of the Seymour H. Knox family.)

Helen Knox, along with her son Seymour Knox III (left), is shown competing in an event known as an Aiken drag. Here, Seymour III serves as the whip for the Aiken hounds. Many other notable families competed in riding and polo events with the Knoxes. These included W. Averell Harriman and Charles Cary Rumsey. (Courtesy of the Seymour H. Knox family.)

Incorporating part of an already existing pre-1890s stable on the Knox property, this stable was constructed in 1917. That original barn housed Seymour Knox's trotters. One of his well-known champion horses was the Red Abbe who used to race at the old Jewett track in East Aurora. There was quite a healthy competition between the Jewett, Hamlin, and Knox farms in those days. (Photograph by and courtesy of Elizabeth Wallace.)

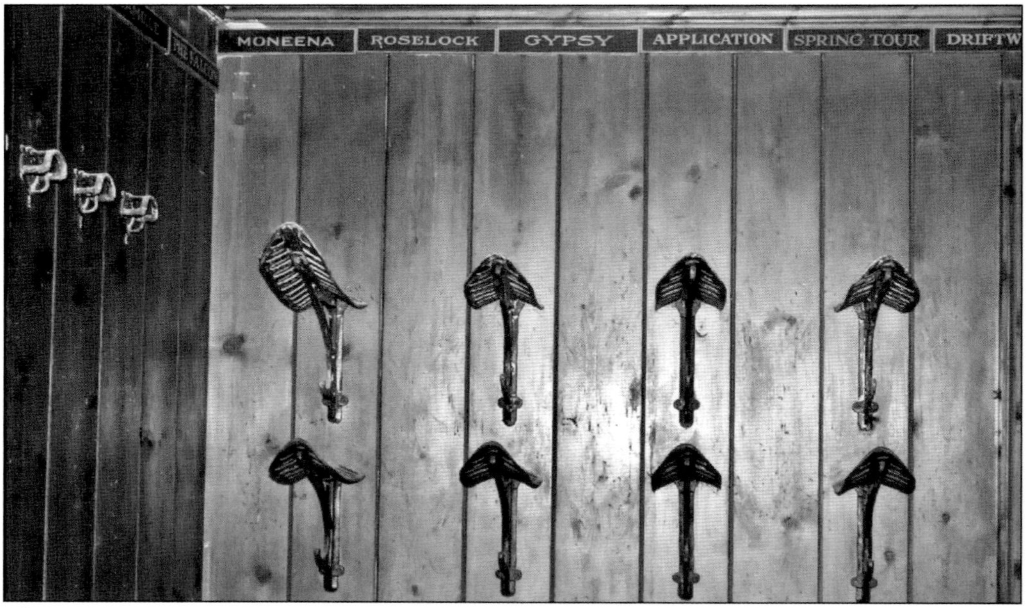

The tack room stored all the saddles and horse-related equipment. After hunting with the hounds at foxhunts on cool autumn days, participants would gather around the fireplace. The nameplates that form a decorative border along the ceiling are the names of all the horses owned by the Knox family and used in competitions. Pictured are the saddle racks designed for English riding gear. (Photograph by and courtesy of Elizabeth Wallace.)

The main polo stable has 36 stalls. Each stall is 12 by 12 feet and has a water bowl that has an on-demand mechanism. The horse would use its nose to press a plate in the container causing water to flow in. This is more efficient than bringing water in by bucket. Each stall has a lift window in the upper bars for ease of feeding. (Photograph by and courtesy of Elizabeth Wallace.)

The actual design of this structure was never intended for winter use. Due to the fireproof nature of the materials used, the interior ceiling over the main stalls weeps badly in cold weather. Drainage was directed to an underground pipe system. A unique feature of the main aisle in the barn is the cork-bricked floor, which was easy on the horses' hooves. (Photograph by and courtesy of Elizabeth Wallace.)

Looking over the greenhouse, this is a view of the main horse buildings. To the left of the greenhouse is a maintenance shed. Most of the help lived in quarters to the west end of the horse barn on the second floor. Knox Jr. demanded that the horses be attended around the clock. Mary Glenn, who worked in the stables in the 1980s, moved in with her children for several months one winter to accommodate Knox's wishes. (Photograph by and courtesy of Peter Potter.)

The farthest right horse and the Spaniel stand on a pathway that led from the end of the polo stables down to the polo fields. The pathway no longer exists. The second-floor loft of the stables was not used for hay or straw. The hay was trucked over to the barn in a very labor-intensive process. Former employees on the farm who were in charge of the horses recall that the barn had no insects, did not smell, and was exceptionally clean. (Courtesy of the Seymour H. Knox family.)

The children of the Knox family were introduced to horses at a young age. Seymour Jr. was a child when his father brought him to a Wild West show at the Erie County Fair in Hamburg, New York, which was about 12 miles from East Aurora. At age 10, his father bought him his first pony that cost $75, including the saddle and bridle. Seymour Jr. said, "If I could ride it back to the farm, I could have the pony." He made it back safely by following his father's trotters. In the image below, Norty holds the lead while Linda sits tall in the saddle. (Both, courtesy of the Seymour H. Knox family.)

Foxhunts, drag hunts, and horse shows all required horses to have good manners, jumping ability, and class. Seymour and Helen were fortunate to be well mounted throughout their hunting days at ESS KAY Farm. Some of Helen's favorite hunters were Pepita, Banner, Tayl D'Or, and Candlebeam. Helen is shown holding a silver award bowl and prize ribbons. (Courtesy of the Seymour H. Knox family.)

An unidentified handler holds one of Knox's championship hunters after competition. Some of the favorite hunters of Seymour Knox Jr. were the Rooster, War Crest, Her Grace, and Echo. Knox reminisces about some of these hunters in his book *Other Tales in Other Years.* (Courtesy of the Seymour H. Knox family.)

This photograph features a mounting table that was commonly used to get up on hunters who can often be quite large. Note that Helen Knox is sitting sidesaddle, which requires an extremely high level of skill to be used in cross-country jumping during foxhunts. The handler with her is unidentified. (Courtesy of the Seymour H. Knox family.)

The original half-mile track was changed into a polo field to train polo ponies. Thoroughbred hunters trained on the farm in East Aurora and at the winter retreat in Aiken, South Carolina. Part of the old Ideal Stock Farm stables was converted into a garage. New stables were built with 40 stalls. (Courtesy of the Seymour H. Knox family.)

The horses are grazing in one of the many green pastures on the property. ESS KAY Farm participated in local fairs, such as the Erie County Fair in Hamburg, New York, in August of each year. Knox also actively supported the local 4-H programs and participated in equestrian events at the fair. (Courtesy of the Seymour H. Knox family.)

The horses raised on ESS KAY Farm for the Aurora team are truly full-sized horses, even though they are typically referred to as "polo ponies." Within the features of their conformation, they are required to be able to run with quick bursts of speed and to possess great stamina with tremendous agility. The horse and his rider must work as a unit. Riders may switch ponies on demand throughout a match; therefore, the ponies must be able to adapt to a new rider. (Courtesy of the Seymour H. Knox family.)

Seymour Knox Jr. wrote extensively on his horses. He notes in his writing that one or two poor ponies can lose a game, the same as a lack of passes on the part of the players or missed goals. A poor pony can also increase the dangers of the game. (Courtesy of the Seymour H. Knox family.)

The Knox family had great respect and affection for the polo ponies that carried them in competition throughout the years. This is reflected by the horses' names displayed on the walls of the tack room. It gave Seymour Knox Jr. great pleasure to reflect back on the color, disposition, conformation, and the natural gifts of these horses. He was able to remember them individually and recount the matches in which they both competed. (Courtesy of the Seymour H. Knox family.)

Pictured here is the Aurora team, consisting of, from left to right, Lewis Smith, Northrup, Seymour III, and Robert Wickser. The match was played on the polo grounds at ESS KAY Farm. Enjoying the activity is Seymour Jr., wearing dark sunglasses, at far right. (Courtesy of the Seymour H. Knox family.)

This image is of the Aurora team based on ESS KAY Farm. As his sons grew, Seymour Knox Jr. was very concerned about their ability to compete at the national level. In 1956, he wrote letters to his sons outlining the training plan to prepare them to compete at national competitions. This insight was gained from his early international training in England and in Argentina. (Courtesy of the Seymour H. Knox family.)

These photographs were taken of polo competitions at ESS KAY Farm in East Aurora. Polo is a sport that requires both the rider and the horse to be extremely fit and strong. Injuries to both the horse and rider can occur even in training sessions. Seymour Knox Jr.'s writings indicate that Northrup was hit in the elbow by one of his own shots, which could have prevented him from competing at the national level. The image below gives a sense of the scale of the polo field at ESS KAY Farm. At these regular events, people watched the match from the tailgate of their car, lawn chairs, or blankets. (Both, courtesy of the Seymour H. Knox family.)

Pictured is the Greentree versus Aurora match on Long Island, the place where polo in the United States began. The history of Long Island polo began in 1879 when several members of the Meadowbrook Polo club started to play the game in the infield of the racetrack of the Mineola Fairgrounds. Members playing included Thomas Hitchcock Sr., Oliver W. Bird, August Belmont Jr., and Benjamin Nicoll. The club was formally incorporated in 1881, and the first official polo field was built in 1884. (Courtesy of the Bert Morgan Archives.)

With consideration that the members of the Aurora team were not full-time players, their skill was equal to those playing at national and international levels. Their goal rankings in 1956 are a good indication of this. Lewis Smith was an eight-goal player, Northrup was a seven-goal player, and Seymour III was a five-goal player. The image shows a spirited match at ESS KAY Farm. (Courtesy of the Seymour H. Knox family.)

Relaxing between matches on the tailgate of a car are Seymour Knox Jr., left, and James Paul Mills. Polo was not a sport without risk. In the fifth period finals at Aurora versus Brandywine held at Oakbrook, Norty Knox fell off his horse, The Queen, and had the wind knocked out of him. He was lucky to have escaped serious injury. (Courtesy of the Bert Morgan Archive.)

This trophy is being presented to the winners of the National Open Championship in 1934. The Aurora team included, from left to right, Seymour Knox Jr., James Paul Mills, (woman unidentified), Elbridge T. Gerry, and Elmer Boeseke. The US Polo Association included 19 clubs in 1894, from St. Louis to Philadelphia. The oldest US polo club is the Meadowbrook Polo Club. The Aurora team participated in other national tournaments such as Oakbrook and Greentree. (Courtesy of the Bert Morgan Archive.)

The Aurora team competed internationally in Argentina in 1932 and again in the early 1960s. Seymour Knox Jr. writes extensively about this in his book *To Buenos Aries and Back, 1932*, which can be found in the rare book room at the Buffalo and Erie County Central Library. The later competitions of the 1960s were covered in *Polo Tales, Volume II*, which was also written by Seymour Jr. The writings indicate that the Argentinean team plays in its native dress, as seen here in these photographs. At ESS KAY Farm, polo matches were not too strenuous and not particularly dangerous, as games were four or five periods. However, tournament polo is much harder and can be extended to six or eight periods. (Both, courtesy of the Seymour H. Knox family.)

In preparation for polo at ESS KAY Farm, the stable workers would turn the horses out after their morning exercise during the summer then bring them in the following morning, except when matches were held. Seymour Jr. felt that, in this manner, they exercised more in the pasture, reducing stable work. Knox indicates that it was his practice not to shoe the horses on their rear hooves to reduce injuries from kicking. (Courtesy of the Seymour H. Knox family.)

This photograph shows polo ponies being walked through the gate near the guest stables at ESS KAY Farm. Close at the heels of one of the ponies is a small dog. Visitors to the park will find that the chimneys on the guest stables have been reduced in size. (Courtesy of the Seymour H. Knox family.)

On the farm there was a clear distinction between the farmworkers and those who worked in the stables. It was considered a step up to work in the stables. Sometimes it required traveling long distances, both domestically and overseas, to care for the horses that meant so much to the Knoxes. (Courtesy of the Seymour H. Knox family.)

Keeping the polo ponies fit for competition was always a challenge, and as the ponies aged, sometimes other friends and owners would lend the Knoxes their ponies for competition. This reflected the great trust and friendship between the Knox family and other notable people who played polo in its golden age in the United States. (Courtesy of the Seymour H. Knox family.)

Six

Working on the Farm

As a self-sustaining enterprise, the farmworkers lived on the property. The stable workers lived either above the stables or across the street, on Seneca Street, in the white houses. The butler's home was closer to town near the traffic circle in East Aurora.

Over the years, there were several farm bosses. Lyman Baker had a farm management background and lived in the green home near the stables. Next were Maynard Pangborn, Roy Rogers, and Luther Lawton.

Fred Kelley served as a groom and helped build the stables. One of Fred Kelley's duties was to clean off the ice on the pond when the Knox boys, Seymour III and Northrup, returned from Yale. Northrup sometimes baled hay if the workers needed a hand.

Fred Kelley's grandchildren Ruth and Mary Bowen remember the Knox family's generosity and friendliness toward everyone on the farm. Northrup taught one of the Bowen cousins how to swim in the pool. The Knoxes handed down their swing set to the Bowens. All the children received Christmas presents from the Knoxes. Ruth and Mary received dolls and Dick a cowboy suit. Another toy they were given was a painted burlap general store.

The Bowen children used to play in the barns behind the house, one of which now houses the carriages. The girls were not allowed to walk in the "big woods" close to the "big house." Mary did not like to walk by the show barn, as the foxhounds' barking scared her. They remember Northrup and Lucetta Knox being very involved with the farm on a daily basis.

Paul Amos worked in the stables and travelled to Argentina when the Aurora team went there. His wife, Annie, was from Scotland, and since she traveled with the Knoxes to Aiken, South Carolina, in the winters, she was never in one place for more than six months, making it difficult for her to qualify for US citizenship. Upon hearing this news, Seymour Jr. intervened on her behalf, and she received her citizenship.

The farmworkers had regular baseball games on Sunday afternoons, and there were three teams, the big house, the farm team, and the stables, that played each other in rotation.

The house above is now the Administrative Building for the Knox Farm State Park. Visitors to the park pass by it on their way to the parking area near the livestock barns. The Kelley family had several children, including Emma Ruth, who was born on the farm and later lived in the house up the hill (below). Four generations of the Kelley family lived and worked on Knox Farm. (Both, photograph by and courtesy of Peter Potter.)

A stable manager at the Ideal Stock Farm, Fred Littlewood Kelley wrote this letter to his wife, Mary Walker Kelley, the week he started. In it, he asks her to have their son Dick take the trolley to the farm for work Sunday morning. The letter was sent from the farm to his wife in Springbrook, New York, two miles away, which was quite a distance at that time. (Courtesy of Ruth Bowen Hall.)

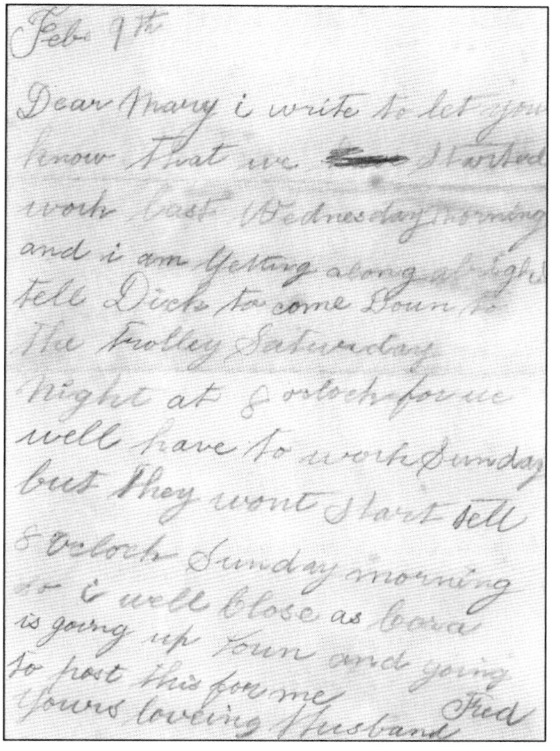

Feb 7th

Dear Mary i write to let you know That we Started work last Wednesday morning and i am getting along alright tell Dick to come down to the trolley Saturday night at 8 oclock for we well have to work Sunday but they wont start tell 8 oclock Sunday morning so i well close as Cora is going up town and going to post this for me

Yours loving Husband Fred

This photograph shows Fred's wife, Mary Walker Kelley, and their youngest daughter, Marie, at the house on the hill. The house, one of the more ornate of the farmworkers' homes on the property, is still recognizable with its white columns and beaded trim on the porch roof. (Courtesy of Ruth Bowen Hall.)

One summer day, Seymour Knox Jr. and Northrup Knox went to town to buy ice cream for Dick and Mary Bowen. They gave the little kids the ice cream then photographed them eating it. Sey and Norty printed the pictures and gave them to Mary, writing "Knox Photos" at the lower right. (Courtesy of Mary Bowen Ess.)

This photograph was taken at the Railway Express Office near the train viaduct in East Aurora. From left to right are (first row) Gordon Amos and Ruth Bowen; (second row) Dick and Mary Bowen. This office would have been located near Riley Street Station, and the train cars can be seen in the background. (Courtesy of Ruth Bowen Hall.)

In winter, the horses would be walked from the farm, down local streets, to Riley Street Station. There they would be boarded onto train cars for their journey to Aiken, South Carolina, to the Knoxes' winter home. This process was also used for trips to New York City for polo matches held on Long Island. Later, a large tractor-trailer was stored in a barn near the guest stable at ESS KAY Farm. This was used to provide a more efficient method of transport for the Aurora team ponies. For example, the Aurora team shipped 18 ponies from East Aurora to Hinsdale, Illinois, with tack, stable equipment, mallets, and the players' riding clothes. The whole operation was quite an expedition. (Both, courtesy of the Seymour H. Knox family.)

The farmhouse can still be seen on the farm from Seneca Street, directly across from Mint Meadow Drive. Once, Gus Walker was painting the farm buildings from the original grey to red with white trim. When he went inside the house to have lunch, a young Ruth Bowen thought she would help out with the painting by mixing the red and white paint together. Farms traditionally painted buildings red to help absorb heat in the winter. All the farmhouses, barns, and maintenance buildings were painted red to give it a unified look. (Above, photograph by and courtesy of Peter Potter; below, courtesy of the Seymour H. Knox family.)

These men were clearing the elm trees that had died either from disease or from being blown down by a storm. The workers are driving a red Farmall tractor model M, which was nicknamed "M." Knox was heartsick at the loss of these trees, as they were integral to the natural landscape design created by Ellen Biddle Shipman. (Both, courtesy of the Seymour H. Knox family.)

According to the records, many of the pastures were named after family and farmworkers. The image above shows a farmworker walking in the Seymour pasture that leads down toward the ponds. The image below shows a holding corral where the cows would be gathered prior to sales. The workers in these images are unidentified. (Both, courtesy of the Seymour H. Knox family.)

Mary and Ruth Bowen recall that, located near the stables, there was a judging stand that was taken down by a tornado. This small building appears to the right of the main stables near the polo field. The small white building to the left is the guest stable. (Courtesy of the Seymour H. Knox family.)

Lewis Smith (center) was the stable manager at ESS KAY Farm and an accomplished seven-goal polo player, as of 1956. Lewis would give Mary and Dick Bowen a dollar to wipe down the polo ponies. Dick Bowen walked the polo ponies to cool them down during and after matches and also turned the scorecards when a team made a goal. Mary helped Annie Amos spring clean in the big house during Seymour's later years and remembers how he loved having his dogs with him. (Courtesy of the Seymour H. Knox family.)

Each summer, ESS KAY Farm hosted an annual picnic for their employees. Here, they are enjoying a fine summer day. In the background are the guest stable and the pasture beyond. ESS KAY Farm provided many individuals with jobs that they may only have had for one or two seasons. However, some worked for the farm for decades and became very close with the Knox family. In speaking with them, one can sense the significance of ESS KAY Farm in their lives. (Both, courtesy of the Seymour H. Knox family.)

Seven

Events, Friends, and Family

The ESS KAY Farm has hosted a wide variety of events, games, and celebrations for the Knox family, friends, and business associates throughout the four generations. Specifically, the East Aurora Hunt and Trials, which began in the 1930s, is legendary in the history of East Aurora. Some remember attending the hunts as children in the time when horses were a major aspect of their recreation and even ridden daily to school in the surrounding communities.

Equestrian activities have always been a major part of the lifestyle of the farm and echoed that of the surrounding community. In the past decade, Knox Farm State Park has evolved into an epicenter for horse enthusiasts with its affiliation with the Equestrian Center on the other side of Knox Road, which is the southern boundary of the park. Also, park activities for the general public have involved interactive experiences for children with llamas, sheep, and miniature horses.

In the early 1960s, the newly formed Buffalo Bills football team was invited to use the ESS KAY Farm as its training and practice field. Living accommodations were arranged for the players at the historic Roycroft Inn in the village of East Aurora. Their equipment was stored at the local high school, and the team was bussed to daily practice. This was quite a novel event for both the team and ESS KAY Farm staff.

With the natural settings of the farm as a backdrop, the East Aurora Driving Society, founded in the 1970s, was invited to host carriage events and competitions during this time. This was a fitting activity for ESS KAY Farm due to the collection of buggies, carriages, and sleighs stored in the large dairy barn. As in earlier times, these events became major social events for both participants and the local community. Carriage drives through the streets of East Aurora gave the opportunity to view and appreciate the variety of styles of horse-driven vehicles used before automobiles became the preferred means of transportation.

This late-1930s aerial view is of Buffalo Road at North Star Road just west of ESS KAY Farm. The image shows the original North Star Tavern with the stables on the property at lower right. Across the road (south), the Taber Earl Tavern is visible; it was dismantled in the late 1940s. (Courtesy of John Davidson of the North Star Tavern.)

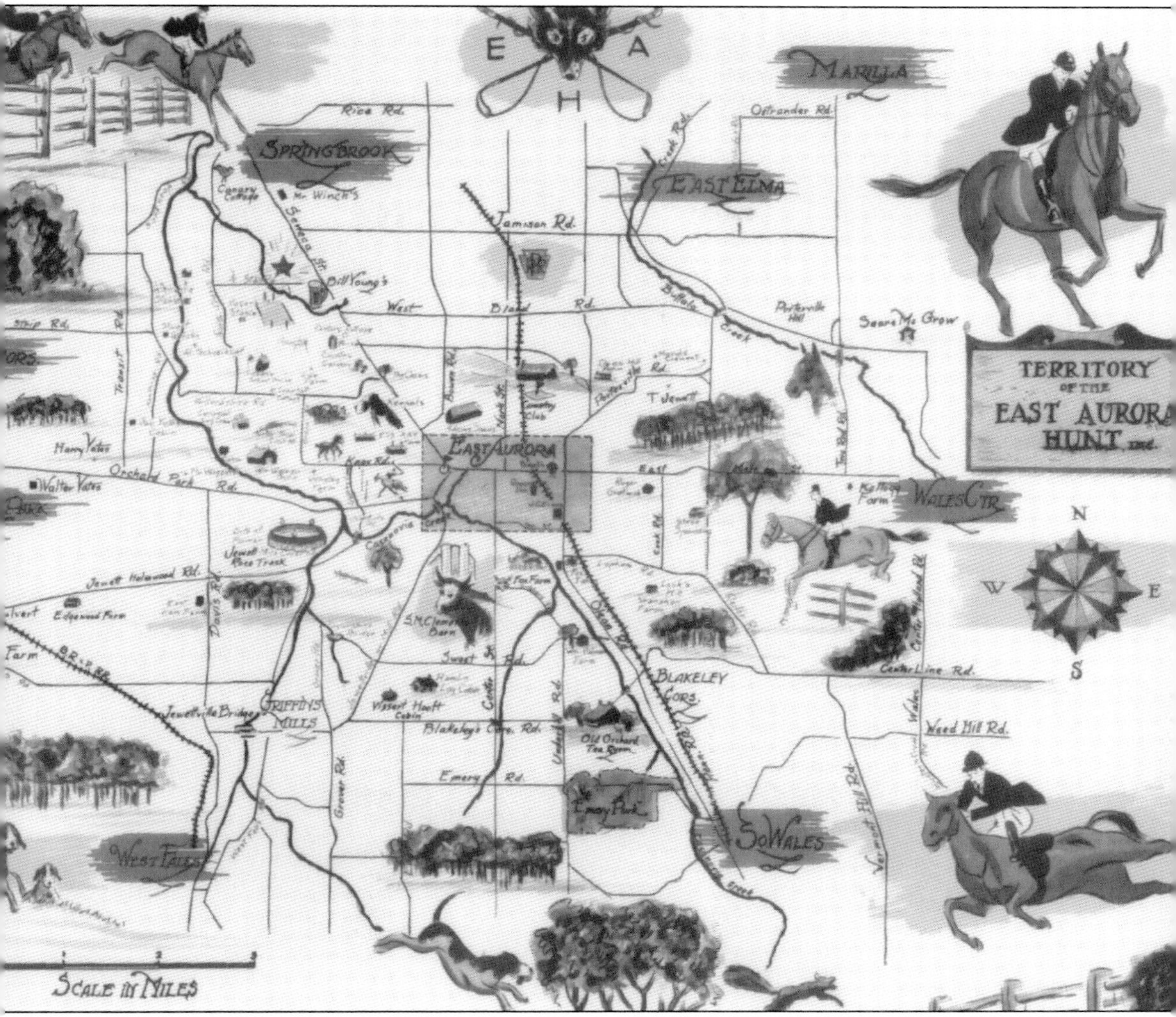

The North Star Tavern was a stop on the East Aurora Hunt. Since 1957, Marie Young O'Brien, who was active in the East Aurora Hunt Club, operated the tavern. Betty Talbott Zink designed this hand-drawn map showing landmarks of the course, the structures, and surrounding communities crossed by the riders. (Courtesy of John Davidson of the North Star Tavern.)

The hunt course extended from Two Rod Road in Marilla to the barns of the 121st Cavalry on Armor-Duells Road in Orchard Park, encircling the village of East Aurora. The riders and hounds could cover more than 15 miles to complete the course. (Courtesy of the Seymour H. Knox family.)

The East Aurora Hunt was a seasonal activity that was held during the years of the Great Depression up to the beginning of World War II. Prior to the East Aurora event, the Lake Shore Hunt Club sponsored events from 1920 until 1930. The hunt season in East Aurora extended from the third week in September until the second week of December. (Courtesy of the Seymour H. Knox family.)

Hunts were held each week on Tuesdays and Saturdays with training runs for young hounds on Thursdays. These were referred to as puppy hunts. The hounds were crossbred between English and American hounds and were maintained in the kennels on ESS KAY Farm. (Courtesy of the Seymour H. Knox family.)

The East Aurora Hunt was classified as a drag hunt. One of the huntsmen would drag a burlap bag containing fox droppings along a course route of his choosing. With the sound of the traditional horn, the hunt would commence and the hounds would pick up the scent trail. (Courtesy of the Seymour H. Knox family.)

An associated East Aurora Hunt riding event was held at estates near ESS KAY Farm during these years. The East Aurora Hunter Trials were designed to show the worth of working hunters over a country course about 1.5 miles in length. Horse and rider would have to navigate obstacles, such as fences of stone or rail and even chicken coops. (Courtesy of the Seymour H. Knox family.)

The East Aurora Hunter Trials were usually held in mid-October with a pretrial picnic at the J. Hazard Campbell home. The owners of the properties used for the trial, as well as their families, were invited to participate in a drawing for a yearling bull and enjoy a greased-pig contest for the children. (Courtesy of the Seymour H. Knox family.)

Holding his daughter Marie's horse is William Young, the 58th owner of the North Star Tavern. Young and his wife, Anna, purchased it in 1922. The tavern was known for its turtle soup; the turtles were raised in the pond behind the restaurant. The tavern was a popular place with the Knox family, who often used it for private gatherings. (Courtesy of John Davidson of the North Star Tavern.)

A 17-year-old Marie Young shows her skills on horseback during a riding event at ESS KAY Farm. Young raised, trained, and owned horses, some of which were kept in the stables on the Knox property. With the close proximity of the respective properties, Young had many fond memories of ESS KAY Farm and the East Aurora Hunt. (Courtesy of John Davidson of the North Star Tavern.)

Helen Northrup Knox, pictured here, was joint masters of the East Aurora Hunt with Cecelia "Peach" Taylor beginning in 1932. Their leadership was a strong bond that helped establish this historical equestrian event associated with ESS KAY Farm. (Courtesy of the Seymour H. Knox family.)

One of the professional huntsmen for the East Aurora Hunt was Paul Yull. Records indicate his years of participation from 1932 to 1939. Yull is remembered as a wonderful person and skilled huntsman. He also worked in the greenhouse on ESS KAY Farm. Tragically, his horn was silenced after succumbing to polio. (Courtesy of the Seymour H. Knox family.)

The hunt season ended with the annual East Aurora Hunt Ball. It was a celebration for both the huntsmen and the farm owners who graciously shared their lands to help make the hunt possible. This celebration was held at the Oasis Ballroom. Foxhunting in the United States was a sport, and the respective members of the East Aurora Hunt wanted the general public to understand that. It was a rigorous, physical, and social event that was attended by many spectators. The members of the East Aurora Hunt were able to experience the natural wonders of the land in a way that was difficult to explain to those who had never ridden in a drag hunt. (Both, courtesy of the Seymour H. Knox family.)

In their inaugural years from 1960 to 1962, the Buffalo Bills practiced on the fields at ESS KAY Farm. During these training sessions, the team was housed at the Roycroft Inn in East Aurora and bussed to practice each day. This 1961 photograph features quarterback Johnny Green handing off to halfback Wray Carlton. (Photograph by Ron Moscati, *Buffalo Courier-Express*; courtesy of Special Collections, Butler Library, State University College at Buffalo.)

Many former Bills players and fans fondly recall these early years of the new franchise. This photograph, taken in 1961, shows Most Valuable Player LaVerne Torczon, a defensive end out of the University of Nebraska. (Photograph by Ron Moscati, *Buffalo Courier-Express*; courtesy of Special Collections, Butler Library, State University College at Buffalo.)

Jack Braithwaith and whip-and-groom Tyler Puddy of Ontario, Canada, are pictured as they drive through the main gate on the Knox Farm State Park. Braithwaith's Oldenberg horse is hitched to an antique Stanhope Phaeton. Dr. George Cormack sponsored this entry in 2005. (Photograph by and courtesy of Dean Miller.)

Gerald McCallum of Tottenham, Ontario, Canada, drives his four to a roof-seat break built about 1900 by the Binder Company of Paris. The team consisted of Dino and Jake, Arabian leaders, and Patty and Muffy, Connemara wheelers, in this photograph taken on Knox Farm in 1984. (Photograph by and courtesy of Dean Miller.)

The East Aurora Driving Society held their annual Carriage Driving Event on Race Day Weekend. Traditionally, it was held on the last weekend of July in conjunction with reunion weekend, when alumni of East Aurora High School gather together to visit. Race Day Weekend hosted a charity polo match and carriage driving events that were attended by residents and visitors from near and far. (Photograph by and courtesy of Dean Miller.)

Don Sutton, whip, is seen driving his Arabian horse–drawn carriage from the ivy-covered carriage barn at the end of the main horse stable at Knox Farm State Park in 2005. For several years, the carriages drove through the streets of East Aurora attracting spectators along the route. Due to a horse mishap in traffic, the carriage drive was then relocated back onto Knox Farm. (Photograph by and courtesy of Dean Miller.)

Knox Farm State Park's 633 acres are made up of a variety of habitats, including woodlands, grasslands, ponds, and wetlands. Hiking, cross-country skiing, horseback riding, and driving a carriage are all activities that can be enjoyed when visiting the park. Don and Margaret Steg of Geneseo, New York, display their skills driving a pair of Welsh ponies in a two-seater carriage near one of the pastures at the park. (Photograph by and courtesy of Dean Miller.)

Carol Moskowitz, whip, and passenger Elizabeth O'Donnell put Oakcreek, a Morgan horse, to a c. 1885 tub-cart on the Knox Farm. It is the entry of Taylorshire Farm, Grover Road, East Aurora. (Photograph by and courtesy of Dean Miller.)

Jean Knox hosted a charity event called A Day in the Country, sponsored by the Association for the Research of Childhood Cancers. Guests were able to enjoy carriage rides around the scenic property. Here, Tyler Puddy of Harron, Ontario, Canada drives his team of Welsh ponies accompanied by his sister Evan Victoria in 1990. (Photograph by and courtesy of Dean Miller.)

Dean Miller, whip, with his daughter Marcia Miller, drives his 1920 Canandaigua roundabout carriage along the Carriage Barn Road on the Knox Farm in 1977. They were participating in the second East Aurora Driving Society event. (Photograph by and courtesy of Dean Miller.)

Pictured is the presentation of the Grand Champion Trophy by Seymour H. Knox Jr. on the Knox Field during the 1984 East Aurora Driving Society event. Standing from left to right are Marge Borchert, Margaret Steg, Don Steg, Seymour H. Knox Jr. (holding trophy), and Elizabeth O'Donnell. (Photograph by and courtesy of Dean Miller.)

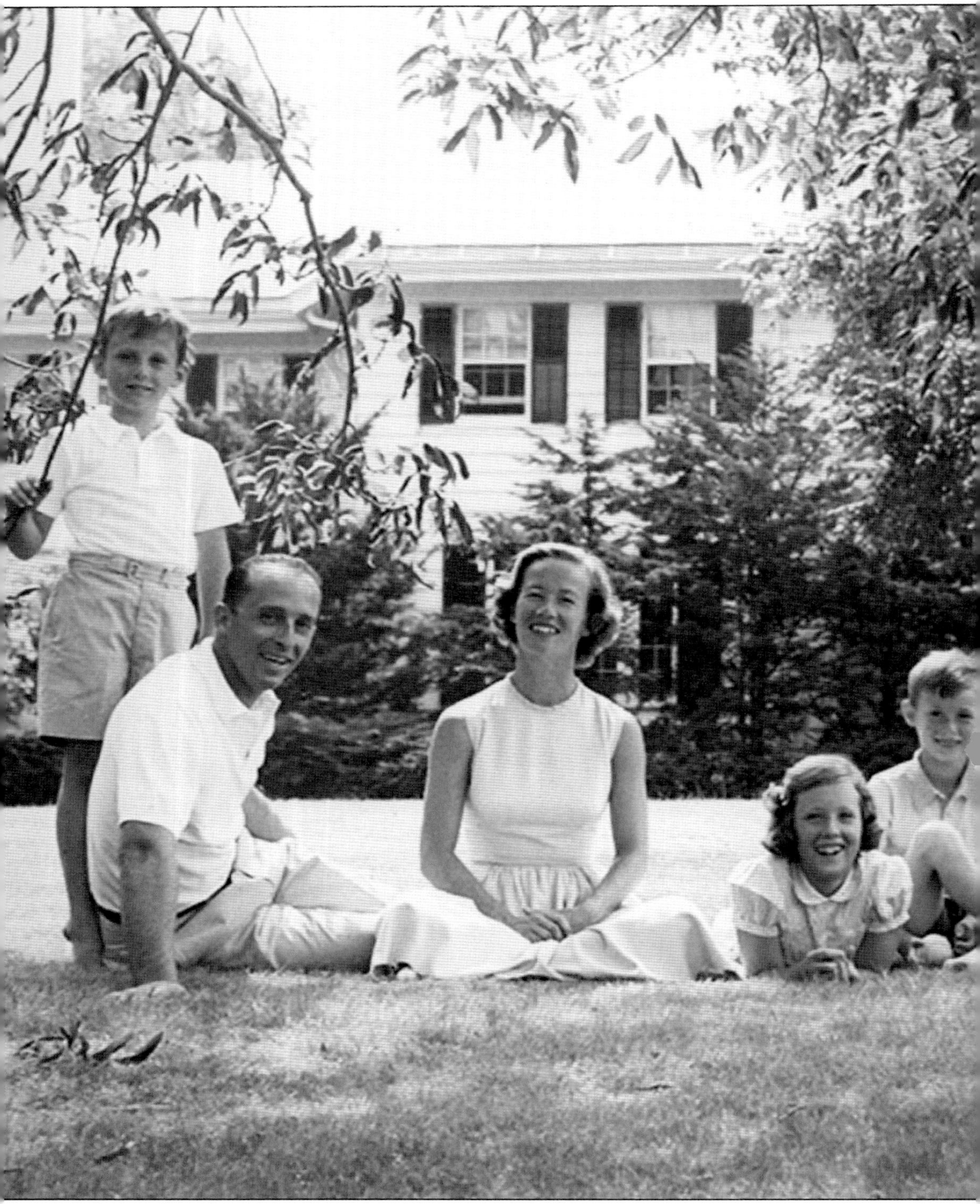

The families of Seymour Knox III (right) and Northrup Knox (left) are seen on the lawn in front of the main house at ESS KAY Farm. Pictured from left to right are Northrup Jr., Northrup, Lucetta,

Linda, Seymour IV, Helen Edith on Jean's lap, Read, Seymour III, and Avery. (Photograph by Elizabeth Kuhner; courtesy of the Seymour H. Knox family.)

The boys Seymour IV, Read, and Northrup Jr. play with a glider on a field at ESS KAY Farm. Seymour IV also recalls the boys riding a go-cart through the woods. The go-cart had a transistor radio attached to it with a rubber band. He also remembers getting a car stuck in the mud in the woods. All the children had favorite places on their grandfather's farm. (Courtesy of the Seymour H. Knox family.)

The boys are playing a rousing game of bicycle polo. Here, they hone their skills for the sport that they would later play on horseback. Currently, bicycling is allowed only in designated areas of the park, and horseback riding is by permit only. (Courtesy of the Seymour H. Knox family.)

Helen with her sons Seymour Jr. and Northrup and the three dogs are enjoying a little fun in one of the family's many vintage automobiles in front of the main house on ESS KAY Farm. Springer spaniels and Labradors are breeds that the family favored for generations. (Courtesy of the Seymour H. Knox family.)

Avery, part of the next generation, sits at the wheel in the family car with the two springer spaniels as passengers. In the background, a boy stands among three grazing horses cooling down between periods of a polo match. The Knox family loved their fine automobiles and their horses. (Courtesy of the Seymour H. Knox family.)

Northrup and Lucetta Knox's daughter, Linda, sits in the driver's seat on M., the red Farmall tractor that was used regularly to help with chores. This young woman would grow to become an accomplished equestrian and a master of the hunt in Aiken, South Carolina. (Courtesy of the Seymour H. Knox family.)

Young Seymour IV and Avery are sitting tall in their saddles in front of the polo barn on ESS KAY Farm. Avery sits on Tommy Hawk, described as a "perfect child's pony." Seymour III and Northrup's first riding and driving pony was Pompano. Betsy (an all-around pony) was ridden by Norty in the East Aurora Hunt and the Aiken Drag as well as for playing polo. Other favorites were Pussy Mouse, Robin Mischief, Carolina, Atom Bomb, and Cougar. Seymour Jr.'s first polo pony, purchased in 1921, was sentimentally named Mardot after his sisters Marjorie and Dorothy. (Courtesy of the Seymour H. Knox family.)

Eight

LEGACY

The establishment of the Knox Farm State Park is the most recent tangible landmark in the Knox family's contributions to society in Western New York. Their preservation of fine arts, support for higher education, encouragement of athletic competition, and creation of buildings to benefit the general population are traced back to Seymour and Grace Millard Knox.

Knox began with his art collection through his affiliation with John Albright who founded the Albright Art Gallery that opened in the era of the Pan American Exhibition. He also was on the board of the Buffalo Philharmonic. His wife, Grace, created her own influence with major financial contributions for the University at Buffalo and the Buffalo Museum of Science. She founded the Junior League of Buffalo in their Delaware Avenue home.

Son Seymour Knox Jr. would take up these efforts with his own interest in art and educational matters in New York State. Knox Jr. traveled widely looking for examples of the evolving trends in abstract and modern art, becoming a major advocate for both the gallery and the artists. He helped to expand both the Albright Gallery's collections and physical space. Thus, in 1960, a new modern addition was combined with the classic Greco-Roman architecture to create the Albright-Knox Art Gallery across from Frederick Law Olmsted's Delaware Park in Buffalo, New York.

Third-generation Knox children follow their parents' example by actively participating in all aspects of arts, education and sports. Shortly before his death, Knox Jr. chose his son, Seymour Knox III to be president of the Albright-Knox Gallery. Seymour Knox III held this position for twelve years before his own death. He was very skilled at raising funds for the gallery and worked at the task intensely. However, Seymour Knox III and his brother Northrup are better known for the founding of the Buffalo Sabres Hockey team in the 1970s. After three attempts to bring a National Hockey League team to Buffalo, the Sabres finally took to the ice much to the delight of hockey fans throughout the Niagara Frontier and Canada. It must be noted that the colors of blue and gold of the Aurora Polo team were deliberately chosen for the new Sabres team.

Grace Millard Knox was the daughter of Charles and Sarah Avery Millard of Detroit. Grace made a generous endowment that contributed to the founding of the University at Buffalo. She was also an ardent supporter of the Buffalo Museum of Science. This oil painting hangs in the University Archives in Capen Hall at the University at Buffalo. (Photograph by Renee Oubre; courtesy of University Archives, State University of New York at Buffalo.)

Grace's son carried on her interest in the arts and in education. This photograph shows Seymour Knox Jr. (at the head of the table) as he sits on the board of the New York State Council of the Arts in 1961. (Courtesy of the Seymour H. Knox family.)

A new annex was made to the gallery in 1962 through the generous contributions of Seymour Knox Jr., his family, and many other donors. Renamed the Albright-Knox Art Gallery, the sleek, glassy, modern wing at left stands in stylistic counterpoint to the classical style of the original 1905 E.B. Greene Building. At the ESS KAY Farm, one could view famous original artworks by masters such as Picasso, Brancusi, Moore, and Still. (Courtesy of the Albright-Knox Art Gallery.)

Architect Gordon Bunshaft (left), Seymour H. Knox Jr., benefactor (center), and Gordon M. Smith, director of the Albright-Knox Art Gallery, look at plans for the new addition. Known for his design of Lever House, the first glass-box skyscraper in New York City, Bunshaft worked in the International style according to the design principles of Ludwig Mies Van der Rohe. (Courtesy of the Albright-Knox Art Gallery.)

Pictured here is the public opening of the Albright-Knox Art Gallery with its new, modern wing. The gallery is a major showplace for contemporary and modern art. During his lifetime, Seymour Knox Jr. donated more than 900 pieces of art to the gallery. Knox personally visited the studio of Clyfford Still and convinced the artist that he should have his paintings in the gallery. The gallery, located on Elmwood Avenue, is situated between Buffalo State College and Olmsted's Delaware Park. (Courtesy of the Albright-Knox Art Gallery.)

The Buffalo Council on World Affairs held its 21st annual citation dinner at the Hotel Statler in October 1980. The dinner honored Seymour H. Knox Jr. From left to right are (first row) David Rockefeller, holding the framed citation, and Seymour H. Knox Jr.; (second row) Wayne D. Wisbaum and Warren Emblidge Sr. (Photograph by Joe Traver; courtesy of *Buffalo Courier-Express* Collection, Special Collections, State University College at Buffalo.)

Nine

A Jewel in the Country

On June 14, 1996, Jean R. Knox, wife of the late Seymour Knox III, and her son, Seymour H. Knox IV attended the dedication of the Russell Town Hall in Russell, New York. Seymour H. Knox, who was born in Russell in 1861, had donated the site to the town in 1917. At the gathering, Jean Knox and her son met J. Winthrop Aldridge, New York State Deputy Commissioner of Historic Preservation. Aldridge suggested to Jean Knox to speak to the then New York State Commissioner of Parks, Bernadette Castro. Following an invitation by Jean,the commissioner subsequently visited Jean at her family's Adirondack camp. A year later, the commissioner came to Buffalo and visited Jean at ESS KAY Farm in East Aurora. During her tour of the property, the commissioner said that "this is such a beautiful place!" This emotional response, often expressed by many first time visitors, stimulated the discussion of preserving the farm as a park.

It had always been important to Seymour Knox III and his family to preserve the 633-acre estate as it had been during the years that they had lived there. Consequently, when Commissioner Castro suggested that the estate would make a beautiful park, Jean agreed. After she conferred with Northrup Knox, who had lived on the property for many years, he agreed also. So in 2001, the Knox family sold the estate to the State of New York so that the public could enjoy the farm as the family had for generations.

Friends of Knox Farm, Inc., is a 501 (c) 3 not-for-profit organization whose members are personally dedicated to protect the buildings and other resources of Knox Farm State Park. The group was founded by Seymour H. Knox IV and Jean R. Knox in 2001.

The Friends' mission is to promote, support, and preserve the natural habitats, green space, and the historic character of the park. The Friends actively encourage and support educational programs and events that develop an understanding of the park's history along with a new appreciation for its ecology.

Many visitors come to stroll, run, or walk their dogs along the fences and the wooded roads that traverse the rolling hills. Often, individuals gaze into the windows of the buildings. Maybe they wonder what it would have been like to live in such a splendid home. These images are the stuff that dreams are made of. Perhaps they are similar to those of the man who came here from Russell, New York, all those years ago.

This photograph shows Seymour Knox Jr. in his beloved 1920 Rolls-Royce roadster, the Silver Ghost. Mr. Knox lived a very full 92 years. He was a wonderful grandfather, who loved driving his grandchildren around the farm in this car or his golf cart. This included driving the children down to the barns to get fresh brown eggs for breakfast! Had he not survived the crash of the Curtiss F-plane in 1917, the lives of the family members and ESS Kay farm would have been much different. With multiple visits to Knox Farm State Park, guests may begin to grasp the scope of Seymour's grand vision of the family's property. (Courtesy of the Seymour H. Knox family.)

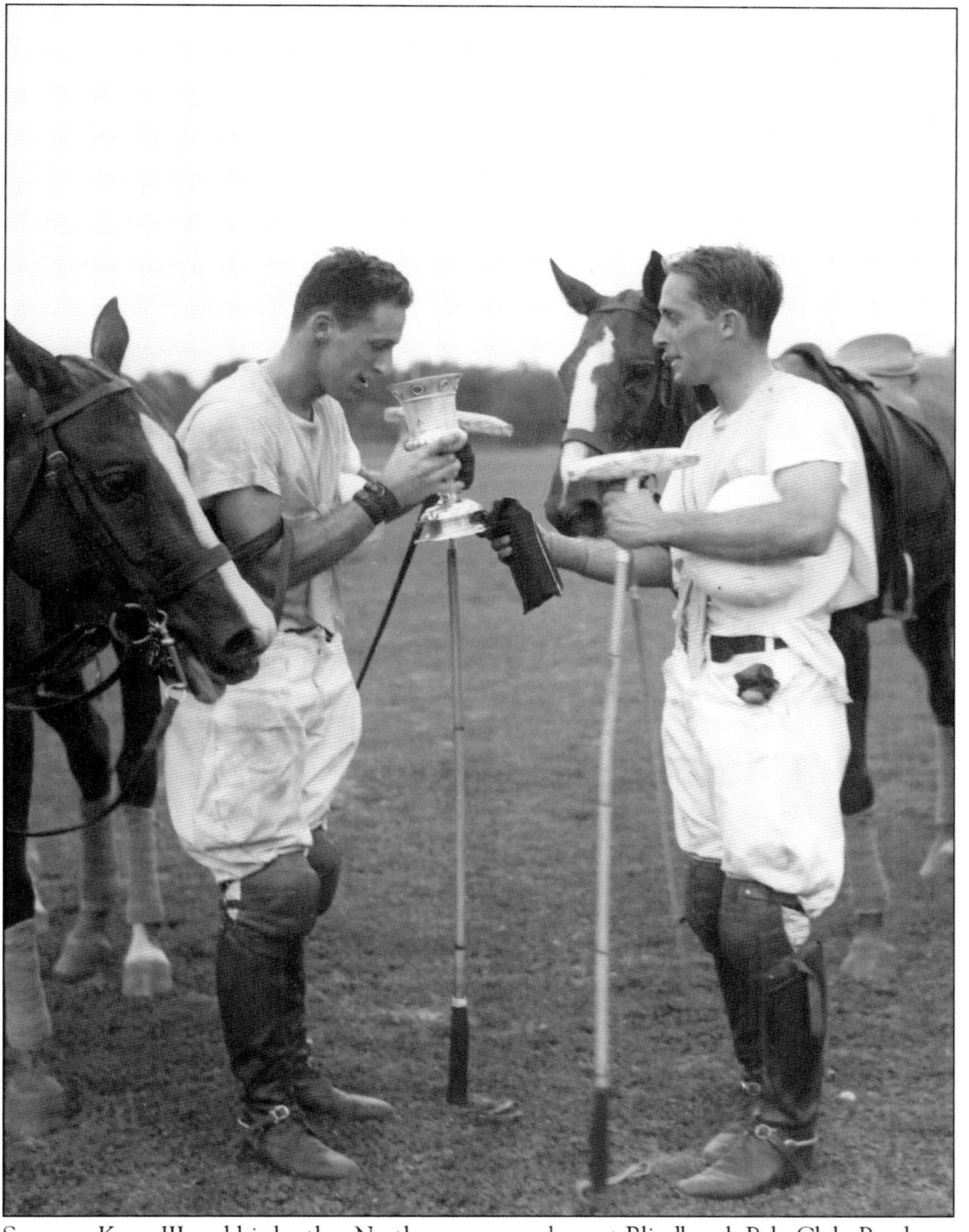

Seymour Knox III and his brother Northrup are seen here at Blindbrook Polo Club, Purchase, New York, after winning the 20-goal polo tournament. Together they succeeded in all their various business, cultural, and sporting endeavors. Their signature legacy was the establishment of a National Hockey League team, the Buffalo Sabres. Life at the farm played an important part in their development for love of the outdoors and sportsmanship. These aspects in the character of the Knox family, along with an inherent tradition of community service, has resulted in the creation of Knox Farm State Park. (Courtesy of the Seymour H. Knox family.)

This lovely tree-lined road leads to the main house and is ablaze with golden color in the fall. On any given day, one finds people walking on the scenic path with a friend or their trusty dog. The park elevates the quality of life of those who frequent it by giving them a natural retreat within easy reach. (Photograph by and courtesy of Jeanne Viger.)

Here is the maintenance repair and storage shed. This unheated shed with its dirt floor was used to store farm equipment and machines on ESS KAY Farm. It was converted by the Knox Farm State Park for similar purposes. It is now a repair shop that is heated and has a concrete floor. Maintenance as well as restoration is a major focus of park employees. Many of the original stone foundations are deteriorating from weather and age. The park's carpenters are seeking to understand how the farm buildings were constructed in order to refurbish them to their original style. (Photograph by and courtesy of Jean Read Knox.)

Helen Northrup Knox leans back against the pillared balustrade, enjoying a fine sunny day with her dogs. Jean remembers that Helen was always beautifully put together whether gardening or acting as hostess for her many obligations in all of her homes. She handled a tremendous amount of responsibility with elegance and grace. (Courtesy of the Seymour H. Knox family.)

A flock of geese inhabits the snow-covered lawn in front of the main house. One may appreciate the grandeur of the main house in this beautiful natural setting. Although built on a large scale, the house evokes a feeling of warmth and refinement due to the personal touches of the family. (Courtesy of the Seymour H. Knox family.)

East Aurora is located in the snow belt of the southtowns in Western New York. These two images show the ESS KAY Farm in wintertime. Both of them contain architectural features of the farm that sadly no longer exist. In the above photograph, one sees the long team barn that has since been torn down due to the deterioration of the foundation. In the image below, the famous ornate cupola with weather vane sits atop the horse stable. The cupola was removed from the barn, and currently, its whereabouts are unknown. The Friends of the Knox Farm State Park are seeking to have the cupola returned to the park. (Both, courtesy of the Buffalo History Museum.)

This brushed stainless steel sculptured fountain was designed and built as a memorial to Seymour Knox III by his widow Jean. Toronto-based artist Manny Neubacher designed it. It was fabricated onsite by the artist along with Joe Houge, James Gifford, and Roy Potter. The fountain is a room of water; one can sit inside it with water flowing all around. It is located near the grassy terrace between the main house and the pool. Paired with the fountain is an abstract sculpture of words, cut with concentric rippling forms. (Photograph by Jean Knox; courtesy of the Seymour H. Knox family.)

These Henry Moore sculptures in bronze graced the lawn near the Shipman gardens on the way to the pool. An avid collector of modern art, Knox Jr. hosted internationally recognized artists at his home on ESS KAY farm. His daughter-in-law, Jean Knox continued this practice. One of her visiting artists was Cole Weston, son of the photographer Edward Weston, who gave a workshop on the grounds at the farm and taught classes at the Nichols School in Buffalo, New York. It is interesting to note that Seymour Knox Jr. had attended Nichols School as a young boy. (Courtesy of the Seymour H. Knox family.)

One cannot think of Knox Farm State Park without envisioning horses. Throughout history, the horse has not only helped shape people's lives but also nations. Truly, the horse remains within the spirit of East Aurora, as it did when Seymour Knox bought his first stallion for the Ideal Stock Farm. (Photograph by Jean Read Knox; courtesy of the Seymour H. Knox family.)

The Knox Farm tour was able to use Smidgy, the miniature horse, so extensively because he was owned and insured by Sue Collins, a volunteer who stood close by as her horse interacted with visitors. "We had students come out and learn equine care, we had special-needs groups and people from group homes come in and brush him or walk him, learn a little bit about the care of horses, what they eat and how you keep them clean," Collins says. Smidgy would stand patiently while visitors lifted his hooves to brush them clean or listen to his heart with a stethoscope. (Courtesy of Sue Collins.)

Sunlight streams through mist that rises from the lush grass where these birds flock. Efforts are being made to preserve the natural features of the park. Trees that perished from disease are replaced with healthy saplings. Revitalized by skilled gardeners, the Zen garden refreshes its visitors. Daffodil bulbs planted on the lawn surrounding the main house renew the flowering landscape of days gone by. (Both, photograph by Jean Knox; courtesy of the Seymour H. Knox family.)

This photograph of Marie Young on the skyline was selected to enhance the text of a *Buffalo News* article in 1937. Today, the Neil and Barbara Chur Equestrian Center at Knox Farm State Park is located at the corner of Knox Road and Gypsy Lane in East Aurora. The new facility promises to be the hub of equestrian activities for decades to come. (Courtesy of John Davidson of the North Star Tavern.)

This photograph captures the carefree wonder of a child playing in the open spaces of Knox Farm State Park. It is the hope and dream of the Knox family, along with the Friends of Knox Farm, that countless generations of children experience the farm in a similar manner. (Photograph by Jean Knox; courtesy of the Seymour H. Knox family.)

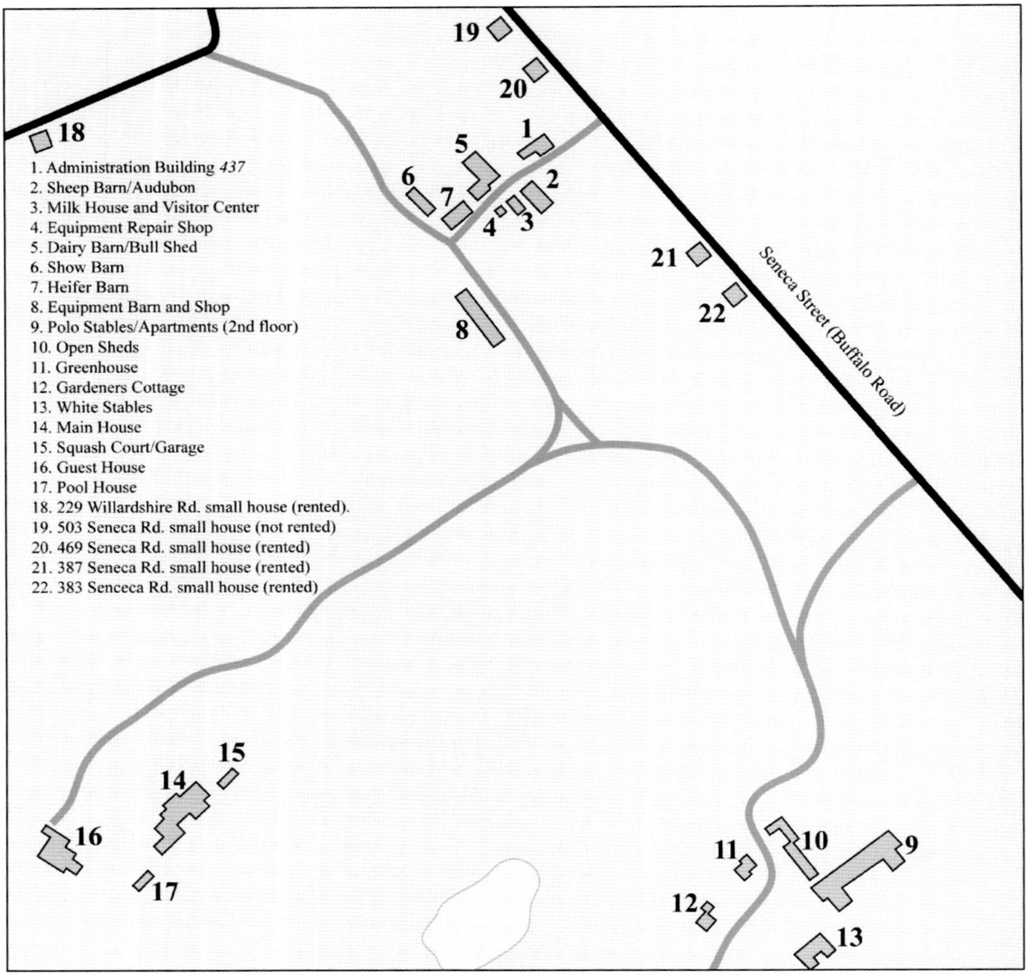

This is a recent version of a map of the Knox Farm State Park used during tours of the grounds. It shows the major features of the park that can be easily followed on a walk along the farm roads. Nature lovers, bird watchers, dog walkers, and people who just like being alive on a beautiful day in a beautiful spot will love this park. The Friends of Knox Farm in conjunction with the Seven to Save and New York State Parks are working toward maintaining Knox Farm as the beautiful place it has always been. (Courtesy of Elizabeth Wallace.)

BIBLIOGRAPHY

Aurora Historical Society. *150 Years in Aurora 1818–1968*. Gowanda, NY: Niagara Frontier Publishing, 1968.

Aurora Historical Society. *Aurora's Architectural Heritage*. Photography by David H. Geyer. New York State Council on the Arts, 1973.

Dayer, Donald H., Harold L. Utts, and Janet R. Utts. *Town cf Aurora: 1818–1930*. Charleston, SC: Arcadia Publishing, 2000.

Knox Jr., Seymour H. *To Buenos Aires and Back*. Buffalo, NY: privately printed, 1932.

———. *Aurora at Oakbrook, 1956*. Buffalo, NY: privately printed, 1956.

———. *Aurora in England, 1934*. Buffalo, NY: privately printed, 1969.

———. *Other Tales in Other Years, 1921–1961*. Buffalo, NY: privately printed, 1971.

———. *Polo Tales and Other Tales, 1921–1971*. Buffalo, NY: privately printed, 1972.

Powell, Karen Plinkett. *Remembering Woolworths*. St. Martin's Griffin Edition, July 2001.

Ross, Donna. "The East Aurora Hunt: Gone But Not Forgotten." The *Chronicle of the Horse*, September, 2008.

Shipman, Ellen Biddle. Personal letters to Seymour Knox Jr. and his wife, Helen Knox. The Division of Rare and Manuscript Collections, Carl A. Kroch Library, Cornell University. 1945–1946.

Winkler, John K. *Five and Ten: The Fabulous Life of F.W. Woolworth*. Freeport, NY: Bantam Books, 1940.

Woolworths First 75 years, 1879–1954 by F.W. Woolworth Company, Copyright 1954.

Consistent with our mission to preserve history on a local level, this book was printed in South Carolina on American-made paper and manufactured entirely in the United States. Products carrying the accredited Forest Stewardship Council (FSC) label are printed on 100 percent FSC-certified paper.

MADE IN THE USA